The New
Careers Concept

LABOR ECONOMICS AND URBAN STUDIES

PRAEGER SPECIAL STUDIES IN
U.S. ECONOMIC AND SOCIAL DEVELOPMENT

The New Careers Concept

POTENTIAL FOR PUBLIC EMPLOYMENT OF THE POOR

Mark A. Haskell

Preface by
Oscar A. Ornati

FREDERICK A. PRAEGER, Publishers
New York • Washington • London

The purpose of the Praeger Special Studies is to make specialized re-search monographs in U.S. and international economics and politics available to the academic, business, and government communities. For further information, write to the Special Projects Division, Frederick A. Praeger, Publishers, 111 Fourth Avenue, New York, N.Y. 10003.

FREDERICK A. PRAEGER, PUBLISHERS
111 Fourth Avenue, New York, N.Y. 10003, U.S.A.
5, Cromwell Place, London S.W.7, England

Published in the United States of America in 1969
by Frederick A. Praeger, Inc., Publishers

Library of Congress Catalog Card Number: 69-19330

Printed in the United States of America

PREFACE

The level of employment, in the aggregate, is
determined by the level of demand for goods and services, private and public, of the nation. Fiscal and
monetary adjustments are the tools through which the
nation endeavors to set a level of aggregate demand
in line with its employment and other social goals.
Fluctuations in employment that follow from changes
in the aggregate demand occur within a number of parameters which vary little in the short run. Indeed,
the way things are produced and the way services are
provided is determined by technology and practice.
In addition, employers, private and public, make decisions regarding allocation of workers on the basis
of a series of judgments about the need and availability of workers of different skill levels as well
as judgments of the kind of worker that can best serve
the various requirements of the institutions and the
work environment.

Thus, the availability of "job slots open to
the poor" is only indirectly and in the long run determined by fluctuations in aggregate demand. In
recent years, economists and policy-makers concerned
with social policy and, in particular, with the problems of poverty have increasingly turned to the study
of variables that more immediately determine who does
and who does not get hired. The rediscovery of the
fact that most of the poor and almost all of those
poor who are employed are unskilled and uneducated
has directed the nation's attention to the qualitative
aspects of the labor force, and we are beginning to
evolve an integrated manpower policy. While not exclusively tied to poverty issues, our national manpower policy is largely geared to the solution of the
problems of the unemployment and the low wages of the
poor.

Project Labor Market, of which this volume is one product, was financed by the City of New York's Human Resources Administration to study the relation between poverty and the job market in New York City, with the specific intent of determining how a labor market policy could and should be developed to help in the eradication of poverty. Carried out at the Graduate School of Business Administration of New York University, Project Labor Market is an example of a larger intellectual and policy concern observable in the work of many other schools and institutions. Although primarily focused on New York City, the study deals with problems and conditions existing throughout urban America, and the analyses and findings need little adjustment to be generally applicable.

Beginning with 1962, efforts at redirecting national resources to raise the quality of the labor force have been increased. This effort is characterized by the passage of acts such as the Manpower Development and Training Act of 1962 and its amendments in 1965 and 1966; the Economic Opportunity Act of 1964, whose Titles I and V provide for training schemes; and the Elementary and Secondary Education Act of 1965. Spurred on by Federal monies, private and public institutions have undertaken to upgrade the educational achievements and skill levels of the disadvantaged. Such activities will not only improve the lot of the poor but also--through the creation of a more productive labor force--make the nation more competitive. In addition, training has salutary side effects: by reducing relevant personal handicaps in dress, speech, manners, and attitudes, it contributes to a reduction of discrimination based on deviations from conventional forms of behavior.

Whether current efforts are large enough is more difficult to determine, for hard data on people in the various training programs are difficult to get, and determination of "need" for skilled labor is, to say the least, tricky. From data in the President's Manpower Report for 1968, one can conclude that up to 800,000 people are involved in publicly funded programs; this is not a small figure. Scattered

data on a city-by-city basis show, at least for the
Manpower Training and Development Administration and
Neighborhood Youth Corps programs, little relation-
ship to need or target fulfillment.

In New York City, activities that strengthen
the supply side are needed. The large number of
teen-agers and "dropouts" in the City's population
make such activities particularly important. Yet
even substantial manipulations on the supply side
make themselves felt only after considerable time and
after numerous adjustments in the labor market.

It was also found that in New York City the
majority of the currently employed poor are either
Negro or Puerto Rican. For them, upgrading of educational achievements and the acquisition of higher
skill levels may not be as crucial as is generally
believed. In many low-wage low-income jobs, the
educational achievements--measured in number of years
of school completed--of Negroes are much higher than
those of whites. In addition, the job-search patterns
of Negroes are much more similar to those of whites
than is generally believed. Much of the preponderance
of Negroes in low-wage, low-skill occupations, therefore, appears to be the result of discrimination,
which is rationalized in terms of insufficient education and skills. Thus, excessive emphasis on training and education may, in view of the persistence of
discrimination in hiring and promotion, prove to be
what is familiarly called a "cop-out." The extent
to which this phenomenon--if it exists at all--is
peculiar to the City of New York cannot be determined.
Surely there is no reason to assume that New York City
is excessively plagued by discrimination; if anything,
the opposite assumption is warranted.

Emphasis on qualitative improvements on the
supply side--and, as a nation, we seem to want results
overnight--implies that the demand for labor can be
affected only in a minor manner, at the margin. In
fact, the reverse is more true. We have greater control over the variables on the demand side. The job
content is determined by the employer, albeit within
technological and market restraints. Changes in job

content are an employer prerogative. Private and
public experience during World War II, when the lame,
the halt, and the blind were turned, with almost no
training or upgrading, into productive workers,
clearly indicates how large is the employer's freedom.

Employer hiring requirements determine who does
and who does not get hired. J. J. Kirkpatrick and
his collaborators have shown, in Testing and Fair
Employment (New York: New York University Press,
1968), that tests employers use to forecast job success and, therefore, to decide whom to hire are
ethnically and class biased, and thus employers' se-
lection tools themselves hurt the poor. From this
type of analysis, it has been argued that employers
require from potential employees the completion of
high school or some other educational requirement
that has no relationship to job content. Clearly,
as average educational level of the population has
grown higher, the educational characteristics of the
employed labor force have shown an even more rapid
improvement. To argue on this basis that employer
hiring requirements tend to be irrational is probably
false; what is certain is that they are undesirable
in terms of poverty reduction. Data scattered in
Department of Labor sponsored studies suggest that
this type of "irrational" behavior is not widespread
in private manufacturing and relates primarily to
times and areas of relatively high unemployment. In
the public sector--in clerical, managerial, and
human-services occupations--hiring on the basis of
requirements that have very little to do with job
content is much more widespread.

The national shortage of public services, in
contrast with the affluence in private goods, seems
to go hand in hand with the fact that we are a
credentials-oriented society. Some public services,
particularly in the provision of human services, are
unavailable because of shortages of properly certi-
fied personnel. Vested interests which are protec-
tive of certification procedures abound and are hard
to dislodge, and job restructuring appears as a solution with much promise. This process, coupled with
the expansion of employment in the public sector--

particularly at the municipal and state level--pro-
vides the basis for the potential importance of cities
as employers of the poor.

Thus, in addition to the new emphasis on training, the recent national concern with the problems of
poverty--as distinguished from the racial problem
with which it is so deeply intermeshed--has generated
three basically new ideas: income guarantees as a
right; the government as employer of last resort; and
the expansion of the number and role of nonprofessionals. The first two appear at this point to be
primarily a Federal possibility. The third can only
be carried out at the local level. Expansion of jobs
for nonprofessionals requires both job restructuring
and at least some training.

In many American cities, the "new careers" movement is well on its way. The passage of the Emergency
Employment and Training Act of 1968, which provides
for funds to communities concerned with removing "artificial barriers to employment and occupational advancement," will help stimulate the creation of new
careers. Whatever the future fate of this legislation,
our cities are moving in restructuring job content and
job requirements to make more jobs available to the
poor within the public sector. It is hard to estimate
how many new-career jobs have been created so far.
Again, city-by-city data suggest imbalances between
new-career-job data and need for them, as well as between program-authorized slots and actual enrollments.
The figures below suggest, at least in part, the
picture--as projected by one Federal New Careers Program as of June 30, 1968, in 12 cities:

	Autho- rized	Actual		Autho- rized	Actual
Atlanta	250	65	Los Angeles	664	737
Baltimore	300	99	New Orleans	250	203
Boston	200	184	New York	1,672	793
Cleveland	250	82	Pittsburgh	200	31
Detroit	140	120	San Antonio	200	107
Houston	250	236	Seattle	30	12

Source: U.S. Office of Economic Opportunity,
         RFP:RPP/E69-20, October, 1968.

The possibility of expanding the role of the City of New York as the employer of the poor through job restructuring has been studied in detail, to establish the potential universe involved and to indicate the necessary steps in the breaking down of jobs into fractions and in their recombination within given service-output parameters. Particular attention was given to health services in view of the general increase in demand for them.

The study's concern with health services will not, it is hoped, be misunderstood and viewed as the only focus of the cities' demand-side adjustments. Dr. Haskell discusses at length the applicability of job redesign to other city agencies. The job-redesign methodology is clearly general. He has also estimated that as many as 25,000 new career positions can be created in New York City. However, since there are no a priori reasons for assuming that the same proportion of positions and vacancies exists elsewhere, this numerical estimate cannot be applied to other cities.

Whatever the potential for new career positions within the public sector of American cities, achieving it will involve a number of agencies and a large number of individuals. City personnel departments will always have an important role, but they alone can never provide the necessary dynamic for job restructuring. In the case of New York, Project Labor Market concluded that the Human Resources Administration, a newly created superagency that coordinates activities in welfare, training, and manpower, should have a major role and responsibility in the area. The following recommendation was made to the City:

> We recommend that the Human Resources
> Administration, in liaison with the
> Personnel Department, assume a major
> responsibility in encouraging job-
> restructuring in all City agencies. To
> do so we suggest that a senior position,
> with a small but appropriate supporting
> staff, be established. In our judgment,
> the person responsible for the job-
> restructuring encouragement function

would be best located directly in the
office of the HRA Administrator.

The specifics of this recommendation are not
applicable to other cities; the general spirit probably is. Job restructuring involves significant
change, and municipal bureaucracies tend to resist
change. Placing the dynamic for change high in the
bureaucratic structure appears to be a requirement
for success.

Job restructuring--as discussed generally by
Frank Riessman and for New York City by Haskell--
implies a "once-over change." This does not mean
that job restructuring takes place in one fell swoop
or that once job content is reset it remains forever
fixed. It is a once-over change in the sense that,
if successful, job restructuring can add as many as
25,000 jobs in three or four years. The process
usually cannot be repeated--and if repeated it cannot
be assumed to lead to further job creation. The question that must be raised then is whether job restructuring re-establishes the balance between supply and
demand and whether it contributes significantly to
the reduction in the number of the unemployed poor.

The answer to this question will, of course,
vary from city to city. The demographic structure
of the nation, region, or city will determine the
answer at least in part. It is clear that the advantages of job restructuring in the public sector of
American cities in the late 1960's and early 1970's
can be assumed to be greater than they will in the
second half of the 1970's, when population pressures
can be expected to lessen. On the other hand, it is
quite clear that job restructuring alone will not
suffice to reduce current poverty levels and will
not exhaust the cities' functions as employer of the
poor.

Dr. Haskell notes the significant extent to
which Federal funds for new careers need to be increased in order for state and local governments to
become employers of last resort. At present, it
cannot be assumed that funds of the needed dimension

will be available, nor can one expect that the job restructuring approach can ever be expanded to permit it truly to fulfill the function of the employer of last resort. Making the city the employer of last resort means that whoever presents himself for work would obtain it, irrespective of qualifications. Only such a scheme would give meaning to the national commitment to full employment.

Project Labor Market has given much attention to the possibility of suggesting to the City of New York that it assume the role of employer of last resort. Our work on this topic has consisted primarily in reviewing the details of a number of proposals developed by Federal agencies and in studying reports developed by private consultants for other cities. A number of basic questions about the advisability of establishing New York City as the employer of last resort remain unanswered; therefore, no recommendation to the City has been made.

Among the questions for which we are searching an answer are the following: Can the government of any one city--the City of New York in this case--take on the commitment of employer of last resort if there is no equivalent commitment for the rest of the nation? Can the City's agencies and departments ever achieve the needed degree of coordination to implement the program? How much pressure on the general level of wages would it create?

The search for a specific affirmative recommendation was encouraged by the fact that if economic conditions continue as they are and if forecasts for the nation's future economic development are accurate, the number of individuals who would actually take advantage of any city as employer of last resort will be small, and costs--particularly if at least some Federal funds can be obtained--will be limited. Furthermore, the permanent introduction of such a scheme would have very large psychological, educational, and income benefits: No one would be able to claim he is unemployed because "there is no work"; there is no better form of job training than working; and there would be no difficulty in specifying the labor requirements for a number of unfilled and needed public services. At present, however, not enough is known to depart from the generally accepted notion that the responsibility for establishing the government as the employer of last resort is Federal.

Project Labor Market and Dr. Haskell's study have focused on the cities' poverty problems, which are among the most serious of all the problems confronting the cities. Job restructuring is presented as a major program for reducing the cities' poverty.

OSCAR A. ORNATI
Director
Project Labor Market

ACKNOWLEDGMENTS

The author wishes to acknowledge particularly the assistance of William G. Chase, Jr., who provided invaluable aid in interviewing and in performing statistical calculations. Mr. Chase also wrote a first draft of a portion of Chapter 2. The author is further indebted to Solomon Hoberman, Director of Personnel of the City of New York, who pointed the study in the direction of health manpower, gave generously of his time, and made available the research materials in his office.

Numerous other persons graciously cooperated in discussing the project with the author and with Mr. Chase. These were Henry Bertran, Dr. Howard Brown, Dr. Martin Cherkasky, A. B. Eckerson, Robert Galton, Dr. Eleanor Gilpatrick, Lydia T. Hall, Dr. Louis Hellman, Cynthia Kinsella, Harold Light, Herbert Lukashok, Dr. Nasri Michelin, Phillip Morgan, Dr. S. David Pomrinse, Dr. Sumner M. Rosen, Dr. Joseph Smith, Commissioner of Hospitals Joseph Terenzio, Peter Terenzio, Dr. Ray E. Trussel, and Dr. Julius Yourman.

Finally, Dr. Oscar Ornati and the staff of Project Labor Market were instrumental in helping to focus the research and to relate it to other of the ongoing studies.

The conclusions and recommendations of this study are those of the authors and do not necessarily reflect the views of the Human Resources Administration of the City of New York or of any other agency of the City government.

CONTENTS

LIST OF TABLES

INTRODUCTION

Although economists assume long-run equality
between the demand for various types of labor and the
skills the labor force offers, in the short run, these
will inevitably diverge. An individual cannot change
the skill he offers as quickly as production techniques
change, and it is the latter factor which is the principal determinant of job content and the occupational
structure. Production techniques themselves reflect
shifts in consumer demand and available technology.
For some individuals, whose occupational or geographical mobility is limited or who never acquire usable
skills in the first place, this "short run" may be
the duration of a working life. The unemployment that
results from the mismatching of the supply of and demand for labor is called "structural," to distinguish
it from unemployment caused by insufficient aggregate
demand and from that caused by the normal "frictions"
of the labor market.

What is to be done when supply and demand diverge? The major process of adjustment has always
taken place and will continue to take place through
the upgrading of the labor force by means of the application of various types of training, whether formal or on-the-job. To supplement this, it is also
possible to take another approach, particularly when
it appears that retraining of workers is an expensive
and time-consuming procedure. Instead of re-educating
the worker to fit him into the existing occupational
structure, in some circumstances jobs can be redesigned
to fit the skills of the labor force.

Time and resources may not be the only problem.
Training schemes may also come up against limitations
of ability. This is not to accept the proposition
that capacity is innate. Although some limitations
may be genetic in origin, it is generally accepted

that what a man can do depends more on home, school, and neighborhood influences and other environmental factors, including the presence or absence of racial discrimination. The average level of capacity is subject to upgrading through the processes of education and social improvement generally, but the average level of capacity at any given time may be said to be fixed. Some portion of the labor force in the lower reaches of the distribution will, for the moment, be able to undertake only that work which requires limited ability. The concept of job redesign is built on this premise but does not limit itself to it. The second important premise is that there is no preconceived limit on possibilities of upgrading under a redesigned occupational structure. Thus, along with a breakdown of complex tasks into simpler ones, there must be a design of "job ladders" and of training programs to enable each worker to move as far up the ladder as his innate abilities permit. What must be stressed is that formal educational requirements cannot be allowed to inhibit the process. By a proper combination of experience, on-the-job training, and formal course work, the exceptional nurse's aide will encounter no artificial or financial barriers on his or her path to becoming a physician.

It is well, however, not to stress the extremes. Were such a progression possible, we would not expect to see very many persons traveling the full path, whether because of lack of ability, ambition, or because of the normal sifting-out that occurs in any competitive process. What should be emphasized, however, is that there will be no "dead end" jobs at all. The steps between jobs can be made small enough and the training opportunities made so readily available that the normal individual could be expected to make significant progress over his working life.

As the result of recent investigations, it has been shown that many opportunities for job redesign do exist, particularly in the public sector of the economy.[1] Less opportunity is thought to exist in the private sector, because of the presumption that

private employers, under the impetus of competition
for skilled workers, make faster adjustments in using
and training the labor force so as to offset the
shortages and high cost of skilled labor. In point
of fact, the job redesign or "new careers" concept
has its antecedents in World War II, when, because
of extreme shortages of skilled labor, many jobs
were broken down into component parts, so that they
could be performed by unskilled workers or by workers
with a minimum of on-the-job training.

Aside from the existence of the opportunity to
do so, there are also incentives for governments to
become more involved in investigating the possibilities of employing more unskilled, presumably poor
persons through job redesign.

First, there is the general incentive of attempting to reduce the incidence of poverty through
direct employment of the poor. Although increased
expenditures in the public sector are usually not
undertaken for the purpose of providing jobs for the
unemployed poor, when we look at the list of unsatis-
fied urban needs, we can see a tremendous usefulness
in doing so. The principal problem is, of course,
finance, not lack of need. For New York City, the
present revenue structure is expected to raise only
$7 billion in 1975; expenditures are projected at
$8 billion.[2] This gap will almost certainly neces-
sitate tax increases, and one can expect that expenditures will be closely scrutinized by taxpayers for
evidence of "waste."

Nevertheless, the public sector will grow and
most likely at a faster rate than the private. In
spite of occasional work-force reductions,* there
will be new employment opportunities in any case.
These should be viewed as career opportunities rather

─────────────────

*In the 1967-68 City of New York Expense
Budget, 1,227 civil service positions were eliminated. Of these, 933 were vacant and 294 were
filled, mainly by laborers.

than merely as new jobs. Although it is not possible
to guarantee that these opportunities will all be
distributed among the poor, it should be possible to
engage community-action agencies, welfare centers,
and other neighborhood-oriented agencies to act as
information centers in steering large numbers of
untrained and unemployed persons into these new positions.

Second, there are now, and will continue to be
in the future, Federal funds available to hire and
train professional aides in municipal agencies. For
example, the Scheuer-Nelson Amendment to the 1966
Economic Opportunity Act provides that the Federal
Government may pay up to 90 per cent of the cost of
jobs that have promotional opportunities. It is estimated that the City may be able to employ about
1,000 persons under this provision. A huge expansion
in Federal expenditure for this type of program was
proposed by Senator Abraham Ribicoff in January,
1967, when he asked the Senate to appropriate $2 bil-
lion for a program "to provide public service jobs
for men and women who cannot find jobs in the private
sector."[3]

The City should be prepared to take advantage
of existing appropriations, as well as anticipated
funds. The best way of doing so is to be aware of
the major opportunities for job redesign in City
agencies and to be prepared to put such plans into
effect.

Third, the City will have an opportunity to
do something about its chronic inability to fill
vacancies in skilled and professional categories.
Although some of these shortages could be alleviated
through higher pay scales, if we accept the existing
financial and bureaucratic constraints, the redesign
concept promises to be useful in that it will increase
demand in that part of the labor market where there
is a considerable amount of slack and reduce it where
unemployment is nil.

Fourth, job redesign is in many ways only a
synonym for increased efficiency, for it minimizes

costs by optimizing the use of plentiful, relatively
inexpensive resources. Competition usually forces
private enterprise to that position, but an ingrained
occupational structure reinforced by civil service
and licensing regulations does not respond quickly,
if at all, to market forces.

For the nation as a whole, it is estimated
that 5.3 million jobs could be created in the public
sector to meet pressing needs, 1.2 million of which
are in the field of health.[4] For New York City, which
now employs over 300,000 persons, no comparable figure
has been estimated, but on the basis of information
developed in this report, it seems reasonable that
between 10,000 and 25,000 new career positions could
be created in a relatively short period of time, depending on the amount of financing available.* On
the basis of budgeted vacancies alone, there were in
fiscal 1965 2,000 unfilled jobs in medical classifications in the Department of Hospitals, almost 800
in the same classifications in the Department of
Health, and 1,200 vacancies in the Department of Welfare. Smaller departments showed proportional numbers
of vacancies, with professional and technical positions
showing the highest vacancy rates. With respect to
their implications for employment, these figures must
be considered to be minimal, since they do not make
provision for improving the quality of public services.
To bring the municipal hospitals up to standard, to
reduce the City's crime rate, and to improve educational performance in the City's slums would require for-
midable increases in public expenditure and consequently in manpower.

Although this paper may be called a general attempt to explore the need for and the possibilities
of job redesign in the entire City government, its
principal focus is on the largest of these--in terms
of employment--the Department of Hospitals. In addition to its size, the Department of Hospitals is particularly relevant as a reference point for this study

---

*See Chapter 4.

because it has the most severe problem of job vacancies and the most pressing need for improvement of
services. In addition, the greatest amount of experimentation with the redesign concept has taken
place in the health field generally, and, in particular, a substantial amount has occurred within the
municipal hospital system itself.

In Chapter 1, the study examines labor supply
and demand factors in the health field generally and
in the municipal hospital system, in an attempt to
explain the reasons for persistent vacancies in skilled
and professional positions. Next, Chapter 2 sets
forth the "new careers" concept and its relevance to
health services. Some of the specific applications
of the concept, particularly in the municipal system,
are examined and evaluated on the basis of their ac-
complishments.

On the basis of this examination, a proposal
for a systematic redesign of the municipal hospital
occupational structure is set forth in Chapter 3. In
addition to a presentation of the methodology, the
implications of such a program for education and training in health occupations are discussed, as is the
effect on professional societies and employee organizations.

Chapter 4 presents data on vacancies in other
City agencies, examines the applicability of the new
careers concept for these agencies, and discusses
the implications of this concept for job creation.

As indicated in the Foreword, this study was
originally part of a larger project conducted at New
York University, Graduate School of Business Administration, under the direction of Professor Oscar A.
Ornati. The study was carried out under contract
number P-900, administered by the Human Resources
Administration of New York City.

NOTES

1. See, for example, Arthur Pearl and Frank
Riessman, New Careers for the Poor (New York: The

Free Press, 1965). In addition, there are numerous
other studies, both general and specific to particular functions such as social work, health, etc.

    2. Better Financing for New York City, Final
Report of the Temporary Commission on City Finances,
p. 97.

    3. The New York Times, January 24, 1967, p. 1.

    4. Technology and the American Economy,
Report of the National Commission on Technology,
Automation and Economic Progress (Washington, D.C.:
U.S. Government Printing Office, 1966), p. 36.

CHAPTER **1** HEALTH SERVICE WORKERS:
SUPPLY AND DEMAND

It is well known that the demand for health
and medical care in the United States has, in the
past 30 years, shown a steady growth, not only ab-
solutely, but also relative to Gross National Product and to population. In 1928-29, for example,
expenditures on health and medical care constituted
3.6 per cent of the national product, in 1954 constant dollars, of $182 billion. In 1964-65, constant
dollar GNP had risen to $614 billion, a more than
threefold increase in real terms, and health and
medical expenditures took a larger proportion (5.9
per cent) of that larger amount. Even in the postwar period alone, the ratio grew considerably--from
4.6 per cent in 1949-50 to 5.4 per cent in 1959-60,
and finally to 5.9 per cent in 1964-65.[1]

In terms of relative growth, between 1955 and
1960, GNP increased by about 27 per cent in money
terms, and national health expenditures grew by just
under 50 per cent. Between 1960 and 1965, the relationship was similar--GNP growing by 36 per cent
and health expenditures by about 51 per cent.[2] Some
of the increase in demand for health services no
doubt reflected a more rapid increase in the cost of
medical care as compared to increases in consumer
prices generally, but the major part of the increase
in demand was a real rather than a monetary one.

For the future, similar increases in health
expenditure are anticipated. By 1975, the population of the United States is expected to exceed 225
million, with an increased proportion of persons
over 65 years of age. Other sources of increased
demand will be a wealthier population better able to

1

afford adequate health care and an increasing governmental commitment to raise the level of health in
the United States. The "Medicare" and "Medicaid"
programs established by the Social Security Act
Amendments of 1965 are by themselves expected to result in a substantial increase in expenditure for
the aged, for welfare recipients, and for a new
category of beneficiaries, the "medically indigent."

The increase in real demand in the next decade
for the services provided by the New York City municipal hospital system is also expected to be substantial. According to one recent estimate, expenditures on the system will grow from $264 million in
1965 to $498 million in 1975 in constant dollars, a
real increase in demand of nearly 90 per cent. In
current dollars, the 1975 estimate is placed at $810
million.[3] Another estimate, this one "conservative,"
places the 1975 current dollar estimate at only $590
million; it allows only a small increase in the use
of municipal hospital services.[4] It is interesting
to note that, because of the new Federal programs,
under this second estimate, City funds would remain
at the 1965-66 level, whereas the Federal contribution would rise eightfold, from $32 million to $254
million.

It should be pointed out that any estimate of
future expenditure for the municipal system is liable
to be hazardous, not only because of difficulties of
interpreting statistical data, but because the future of the system is in doubt.

PROBLEMS OF NEW YORK MUNICIPAL HOSPITAL SYSTEM

For a decade at least, the deficiencies of the
system have been matters of public concern, being
spelled out in various reports and discussed by public officials and others. In general, the problems
consist of inadequate facilities and equipment and
severe shortages of professionally trained personnel
with the exception of physicians and a few technical
categories. Many of these problems can be attributed
to under-financing of the system relative to need,
but there may be other causes at work.

First, the system operates, and in fact was
originally chartered, to provide care for medically
indigent residents of the City. Consequently, the
19 units with a bed capacity of 18,340 are, for the
most part, located in low-income and slum neighborhoods of New York. Furthermore, "between one-half
and two-thirds of the approximately 17,000 beds in
the system are located in facilities that fail to
meet modern hospital standards."[5] Location as well
as the general impression of inferior service and
inferior facilities tend to restrict the use of municipal hospitals to the poor even though the hospitals can provide service to paying patients. Location and the nature of the clientele are also
alleged to be factors which contribute to the personnel shortage, and the personnel shortage tends to
feed upon itself in that professionally trained personnel with options who might not be concerned by
location and clientele might avoid hospitals where
overwork and lack of technical support are prevalent.

Second, and perhaps of more importance, are
the consequences of governmental operation. Tight
budgetary controls and rigid centralized personnel
procedures are said to inhibit efficient operation
from the hospital commissioner down to the lowest-
level supervisors. One former hospital commissioner
believes that under existing arrangements it is im-
possible for the City to operate an effective hospital system. His successor pointed out at a public
meeting that "what is wrong with municipal hospitals
is what is wrong with local government." The hospitals do not function well, he said, because of general financial stringency and because "they are
paralyzed with red tape." As an example of his frustration, he listed 28 agencies that exercise veto
power over hospital plans but take no responsibility
for the effect of their decisions on hospital care.[6]
The present commissioner has his problems with the
City bureaucracy, too. The attempt by Commissioner
Joseph V. Terenzio and Mayor John V. Lindsay to exempt 88 new top-level jobs from civil service control in order to "avert a crisis of staffing and
organization in the municipal hospitals" was labeled
by City Comptroller Mario Procaccino as "a blueprint
for a colossal pork barrel" that "opens the door to

massive political patronage."[7] Three days later,
Commissioner Terenzio's superior, Health Service
Administrator Howard Brown, pointed out that various
state laws relative to construction contribute to
the system's rigidity as well and unnecessarily
lengthen the duration of hospital renovation and
construction.[8]

The most recent reports of investigatory com-
missions support these views. On May 5, 1967, a
panel appointed by Governor Nelson Rockefeller reported that the City hospitals "do not meet the minimum standards of acceptable quality" and require a
massive transfusion of funds beyond the ability of
the City to raise. In addition to "chronic under-
financing," the Commission cited "rigidity in legal
and administrative procedures which impede prompt
decisions and prompt implementation of decisions" as
a second contributory factor to the condition of the
City hospitals.[9]

A second commission, appointed by Mayor Lindsay,
spoke in a similar vein with respect to the pattern
of organization and administration. In its interim
report, it deplored "the present 'fractionation and
dissipation of authority' that make it so difficult
for the City's health officials to use quickly and
efficiently even the limited resources they do have."[10]

NEW YORK AFFILIATION PROGRAM

The steady barrage of criticism has not all
gone for naught. As a result of a commission investigation in the late 1950's, the Hospitals Department
began to extend its program of affiliating individual
municipal hospitals with voluntary teaching hospitals
or medical schools. The individual contracts differ,
but generally they provide that the affiliated hospital will recruit, staff, pay for, and direct the medical staff in return for an annual lump sum payment.
In some instances, other services such as laboratories
and social services are included and, in one case,
the affiliated institution is responsible for the
provision of nursing services.

There is general agreement that the affiliation
arrangements have resulted in dramatic improvement in
the professional medical staffs in the municipal system to the point where they are sometimes on a par
with those in the best voluntary institutions, although the extent of the improvement has varied generally with the strength of the voluntary affiliate.
The Director of Montefiore Hospital reported that
patients at the City affiliate, Morrisania, received
medical care equal to that provided at Montefiore,
but he went on to say that the "antiquated facilities" at Morrisania interfered with the attempts of
the staff to provide such care.[11] In the same vein,
Commissioner Terenzio recently pointed out that the
City hospitals had been able to recruit a slightly
higher proportion of interns sought than the voluntary hospitals from the 1967 graduating classes of
American medical schools. This success was attributed by the Commissioner directly to the affiliation
program.[12]

The newfound ability to recruit strong medical
staffs stems not only from generally higher salaries
and freedom from various governmental restrictions,
but from the fact of the teaching affiliation itself.
With respect to other services, flexibility in budgets, assignments, and salary seem to have been the
most important elements of success.[13]

In the same way that there has been general
agreement regarding the effects of the program on
medical care, there has also been a considerable
amount of agreement that the affiliation arrangements
can only be considered a temporary "stop-gap" because of certain inherent deficiencies.

One group of critics has focused on the steep
rise in costs under the agreements* and alleges that
various abuses have taken place because of the lack
of proper accountability for the use of public funds.
These deficiencies have been very recently set forth

----

*Currently $80 million per year.

in a report of the Institute for Policy Studies that
speaks of "waste, lax administration, patient dump-
ing and possible misuse of public funds."[14]

Another difficulty arises from the fact that
the City institutions sometimes find themselves operating under two personnel and salary systems. Under the agreements, City employees in contracted-out
services have the option of remaining on the City
payroll, but, as they vacate these positions, the
appropriation is transferred to the contract and the
affiliate does the hiring. Similarly, if a City employee chooses to work for the affiliate, the appropriation is transferred.* The result is much employee dissatisfaction, particularly where salaries
and other working conditions vary significantly.

PROPOSALS FOR MUNICIPAL SYSTEM

As a result of the recognition of these problems, three basic remedies have been put forth with
respect to the future of the municipal system.

Transfer to Voluntary Hospitals

One view challenges the very necessity of the
City operating its own system for the poor. Its advocates point out that the institution of Medicare
and Medicaid programs now enables the poor to purchase service from voluntary hospitals of the same
quality as fee-paying patients or those whose fees
are paid by private medical insurance programs. The
logical consequence of this argument is that the City

----

*The following positions are involved in the
contracts with the affiliate: Psychology titles,
Anesthetist, EKG Technician, X-ray Technician, Occupational Therapist, Speech and Hearing Therapist,
Medical Record Librarian, Social Work titles, scientific titles in chemical and bacteriological occupational groups, Laboratory Aide, and Rehabilitation
Counselor.

can rid itself of virtually all medical costs except
administrative ones connected with the Federal and
state programs and improve the quality of care fur-
nished to the poor by turning over the entire physical plant to the voluntary hospitals.

Those who question this solution argue that,
first, the voluntary hospitals have "conceptual
problems" in providing good service to indigent persons.[15] It is alleged that the poor have for so long
received separate and unequal treatment, if the hospitals condescended to treat them at all, that nothing better is likely under a new system.

Second, the critics point out that the govern-
ing boards of the voluntaries are not representative
of the community and are neither responsible nor re-
sponsive to it. One of the strong advocates of voluntary hospital operation, Dr. Martin Cherkasky of
Montefiore Hospital, grants this but argues that the
community can be represented if the City asserts its
responsibility to exercise a greater degree of con-
trol--a responsibility arising from the City's heavy
support of the voluntary hospitals.[16]

On a more pragmatic level, it has been asserted
that even if all the problems are overcome, political
considerations will prevail. Thus, the vested interests and political power of 36,000 municipal hospital
employees could prevent the City government from operating a separate system. It is this political
power that was said to have forced the City to buy
an obsolete voluntary hospital, St. Francis, which
was on the verge of closing.[17]

Decentralization

The current City administration has rejected
the proposed transfer, at least until a reorganization
of the system in the direction of decentralization
combined with the introduction of a modern concept of
medical care has had an opportunity to prove itself.
In addition to those two changes, Health Services Administrator Brown believes that a municipal system
must ultimately provide services for all income

groups, not only for the poor as at present. This
latter point is particularly significant for staffing:
it is said that one of the difficulties of recruiting professional personnel is that many find it un-
pleasant to care exclusively for the poor.[18]

The proposed reorganization would create several new noncompetitive job titles, ranging from
Assistant Hospital Commissioners at $23,000-30,000
per year to Management Staff Specialists at $15,000,
totaling 152 jobs. Each hospital or medical center
would be under the direction of an assistant commissioner who would in turn have the authority to choose
his own top assistants. The assistants would be
exempt from civil service and could be discharged
without recourse to appeal if their work was considered unsatisfactory. And, unlike present hospital
administrators, who are paid up to $18,000 per year
and who essentially act as liaison men between their
institutions and the Department of Hospitals' central
office, the new assistant commissioners would have
the power to hire nurses and other workers, to buy
equipment, to let and direct contracts for renova-
tions, and to make some changes in medical services.
The reorganization would not affect the affiliation
arrangements; rather, it is aimed at more efficient
operation of the City plant and the services the City
operates.[19]

The reorganization is only the first step in
making the City institutions viable ones. Perhaps
even more important in rehabilitating the system and
making it attractive to all income groups is the notion of converting the existing facilities into
"neighborhood health centers." The general philosophy of this approach is that medical care should
not be delivered in "sporadic bursts of concentrated
attention"; rather, health maintenance programs must
be continuing, readily available, and inexpensive.[20]
Furthermore, it is argued that the most effective
method of incorporating modern developments into
general medicine is through the hospitals with their
advanced technology and corps of specialists. In
short, the individual practice of medicine is said
to be "dead" for all but upper-income groups. The

neighborhood concept, embodying as it does a system
of preventative care, is particularly appropriate
for the poor, who have problems of inadequate nutri-
tion and a greater degree of susceptibility to physical and mental deterioration than middle- and high-
income persons.

The New York City approach to this new concept
consists of a general care hospital of 400 or 500
beds as the central operating unit in a center that
includes an ambulatory care unit, an extended care
nursing facility, and a community mental health
center. In addition to reflecting a new notion about
continuity of medical care, the emphasis on ambulatory clinics reflects the fact that demand for out-
patient clinic and emergency services has increased
at the rate of 5 to 6 per cent per year, indicating
"the growing need and demand for personal care of
the kind the family doctor used to provide" and the
fact that "the general practitioner has virtually
disappeared from low income areas" and that "the
hospital has become for many people the only available
medical resource."[21] Further, it is considered that
it is uneconomical to use an expensive resource like
the hospital for services that can be provided at
smaller cost in other ways.

Consequently, the City is planning not only to
renovate and replace badly deteriorated facilities,
but it plans new construction to meet the needs of
chronically and mentally ill persons and is planning
16 new neighborhood family-care centers in low-
income areas at a total cost of $23.5 million. Each
of these centers will be linked to a public or voluntary hospital.[22]

Administrative Reorganization

The third administrative alternative to the
present arrangements is designed to overcome the
objections put forth about the exclusivity of the
voluntary hospitals. Although the proposal takes
various forms, its essence is to place administration of the system or of each hospital under a public authority which, although financed by City,

State, and Federal funds, would not be bound by
normal budgetary and personnel regulations. Ultimate authority would rest with a board of trustees
or "community leaders." In contrast to the arrange-
ment just discussed, this could conceivably operate
without affiliation agreements once the system had
been brought up to par, although at least one version
recommends a continuation or expansion of them.[23]

This alternative seems to be the one favored
by Health Services Administrator Brown if steps cannot be worked out to improve the operation of the
system or if, after all the proposed changes are put
into effect, the system is still not acceptable to a
wide range of income groups.[24]

PERSONNEL SHORTAGES

Although an administrative reorganization of
New York City's municipal hospital system can be
said to have implications for the quality of the hospital care available to City residents, the new
structure will still be faced with difficult recruit-
ment problems in the face of increasing demand for
hospital services. Similarly, even though the City
government may be able to divest itself of the problems of recruiting adequate numbers of professional
personnal of the proper quality by transferring its
hospitals to other organizations, the problem will
still exist for whoever runs them, even though reorganization of administrative functions may ease it
somewhat.

Even under the best of administrative arrangements, short-run demand for skilled personnel will
exceed short-run supply. In addition, there is some
question about the ability of America's health education institutions to supply adequate numbers of
trained personnel to relieve existing shortages and
provide for the rapidly rising demand for health
services in the next decade, even though under recent Federal legislation there has been a steady
expansion of provisions for training professional and
nonprofessional workers for health-related jobs.

Technological change is not expected to provide a significant offset to increased need for skilled manpower. Although it may have the effect of reducing demand for certain types of workers, in other applications the opposite effect will prevail. For example, as a result of significant advances in surgical techniques, it is expected that "an increased number of professional and other health workers trained in new health specialties will be needed."[25]

On balance, it appears that computer technology will have the effect of reducing expected employment expansion among low-skilled groups such as medical records personnel, dietary personnel, laundry, housekeeping and maintenance personnel, and administrative and office personnel. Other forms of technological advance will tend to increase demand for professional and technical manpower. Over-all, when all forces are taken into consideration, there will be an increase in employment in the health service industry in the next ten years of about 33 per cent, just slightly less than the 1955-65 increase. The largest increases, as shown in Table 1, will be in the skilled categories, the smallest in the unskilled, with the exception of pharmacists where "systems utilizing mechanized drug stations, specially designed drug carts for each nurse station and prepackaging of medications for single-dose use, promise . . . labor-saving gains."[26]

With regard to present shortages, the most recent estimates state that 257,000 additional professional and technical and auxiliary personnel need to be added to provide "optimum patient care." This represents an increase of about 20 per cent over present staffing of 1.3 million. The most urgent needs are in the various nursing categories, with nurses, practical nurses, and nurse's aides accounting for 175,000 of the total.[27]

Projected Shortages

Although all estimates of future needs and future shortages are subject to considerable error, there are a number of indications that the manpower

Table 1

ESTIMATED EMPLOYMENT* IN HEALTH SERVICE INDUSTRY,
BY OCCUPATIONAL GROUP, 1965, 1970, AND 1975

Occupational Group	Thousands of Employees			Per Cent Change 1965-75
	1965	1970	1975	
Total Employment	2,700	3,150	3,600	+33%
Medical Laboratory Personnel	100	130	160	+60
X-ray Technologists	30	40	52	+73
Rehabilitative and Other Technicians	120	150	185	+54
Nursing Personnel	1,200	1,415	1,700	+42
Medical Records Personnel	35	39	42	+20
Dietary Personnel	235	265	295	+26
Laundry, Housekeeping, and Maintenance	280	320	345	+23
Administrative and Office	500	570	600	+20
Pharmacists	11	12	13	+18

*Full-time equivalent.

Source: Herman M. Sturm, "Technological Developments and Their Effects Upon Health Manpower," Monthly Labor Review, January, 1967.

problem will continue to be acute in 1975. In the
aggregate, for example, it is estimated that 120,000
new health workers must be added to the labor force
in each of the next ten years to meet rising manpower requirements. This is in addition to those
who must enter the labor force to replace those who
leave because of death, retirement, and for other
reasons. As indicated earlier, the demand for different skills will vary. Among occupations, the
most critical shortages are expected to be among
dental hygienists whose annual output must triple,
X-ray technicians and medical technologists whose
output must increase five times, and occupational and
physical therapists, ten times.[28]

     With respect to physicians, at the end of 1965,
there was a ratio of 153 to each 10,000 persons. To
maintain this ratio, there will in 1975 have to be
352,000 physicians as against 305,000 in 1965. This
goal can be met only if the present rate of influx
of graduates of foreign medical schools continues.
American medical colleges will not by themselves
produce enough graduates to meet it, a situation
largely due to the medical profession's notorious
policy of artificially restricting the number of
American medical schools and the number of students
within them.

     The nation will need approximately 850,000 pro-
fessional nurses by 1975, requiring graduation of
100,000 nurses annually by 1969. At the present
time, the 33,000 nursing school graduates provide a
net addition of only 10,000 each year; more than
two thirds of them leave the profession.[29] The
nursing problem is further complicated by the fact
that the American Nurses' Association has recently
taken the position that the minimum preparation for
professional nurses should be the baccalaureate degree in nursing. This will not only lengthen the
time necessary to produce registered nurses; it may
also eliminate some hospital training programs unless
they are able to affiliate with universities.[30]

     Figures like these are typical of the other
"shortage" occupations. New training efforts are

impressive, but they appear by themselves inadequate
to meet the drastically expanded need--certainly not
within eight or ten years.

Current Shortages

Naturally, the degree of shortage varies among
geographical areas. Rural areas tend, in general, to
be worse off than urban places, but there are great
differences among urban areas and even within them.
In New York City, there seems to be no over-all
shortage of physicians, but other occupations are
understaffed. Even these shortages are not distributed equitably; the City's voluntary and private
hospitals more closely meet their requirements in
professional and technical fields than do the municipal institutions. In the latter, the nursing shortage is most acute, reaching "crisis" proportions in
some of the hospitals. Over-all, the voluntary hospitals are estimated to have 75 per cent of staff
(registered) nursing jobs filled, while the City
hospitals have filled only 35 per cent of their open-
ings in this category. In some City institutions,
the 4:00 P.M.-to-midnight shift averages only one
registered nurse for 100 patients, and the midnight-
to-8:00 A.M. shift only one registered nurse for 200
patients. Paradoxically, in these situations, physicians sometimes perform nursing duties because they
are not in such short supply.[31]

Other glaring examples of personnel shortages
have been pointed out recently in the press, although
they certainly came as no surprise to City hospital
officials. On one evening tour, Commissioner Terenzio
found only 14 staff nurses to 1,108 acutely ill patients at Bellevue Hospital, 5 nurses for 670 patients
at Metropolitan Hospital, and 13 nurses for 719 patients at Queens General Hospital.[32]

On an earlier tour of Bellevue, State Senator
Seymour Thaler found eight operating room nurses
where 32 were said to be needed and no registered
nurses in the neurological ward's intensive care unit,
where there were five acutely ill patients. On the
same visit, the Chief of Pathology stated that

"several important laboratory tests had been discontinued because of personnel shortages," including "certain tests for high blood pressure and steroid tests."[33]

In total, only 275 staff nurses, including those in emergency and delivery rooms, are on permanent evening and night duty in all 19 hospitals to cover an average of 14,500 patients. To relieve this situation, Mayor Lindsay recently announced a $700 annual increase to registered nurses on those shifts and a reclassification of them to head nurse to supplement an existing differential of $900 on the 4:00 P.M.-to-midnight shift and $720 on the midnight-to-8:00 A.M. shift. In the New York Times article reporting these changes, it was pointed out/that night differentials at four voluntary hospitals range from $1,320 to $1,800.[34] Earlier, Dr. Brown had directed Bellevue Hospital to hire 100 additional ward clerks and messengers to relieve the overworked nurses. This in spite of the fact that all 131 budgeted positions for ward clerks had already been filled.[35]

A more unorthodox approach to the problem of acute shortages at night seemingly had forced the issue and caused Commissioner Terenzio to seek increased differentials. Early in 1967, Coney Island Hospital had lured 25 nurses out of retirement with the offer of $39 per shift as against $26 on the technical grounds of classifying them as special-duty nurses when in fact they were assigned ward duty. The funds were available in the budget because this hospital had filled only 17 per cent of its staff nurse positions and had only four registered nurses at night for 500 patients.

When the City refused to pay more than $26 per shift, the nurses immediately resigned. The dispute was finally settled when Maimonides Hospital, the voluntary affiliate of Coney Island Hospital, agreed to provide the additional $13 in the future. The immediate deficit was paid through philanthropic contributions.[36] Coney Island's administrator summed up the episode nicely in a few words. He stated, "I need nurses, so I decided to bend the rules."[37]

For the entire system in 1966, of 8,004 budgeted professional nursing positions, only 3,275 were
filled by registered nurses while 3,696 were filled by
practical nurses, nursing aides, and a few nonnursing
personnel, leaving 1,033 vacancies, but a shortage
of 4,279 professionals. Table 2 shows these figures
as well as vacancies in nonprofessional nursing categories. For licensed practical nurses, 1,258 vacancies are partially offset by the use of 1,108 nurse's
aides and nonnursing personnel. The smallest deficit
exists in the nurse's aides category where there are
4,450 aides for 5,142 positions supplemented by 488
nonnursing personnel, leaving 204 vacancies.

Although shortages in other occupational categories are not so dramatic, they are, nevertheless,
persistent. Table 3 shows, by medical occupational
groups for fiscal 1965, the numbers of employees actually on the payroll, budgeted positions, and
vacancies for the City hospitals.

In addition to these civil service occupational
groups, there were a number of individual job classifications in which there were some large disparities
between budgeted and filled jobs. There were, for
example, 15 dentists for 47 positions, 345 interns
for 452 positions, and 1,388 residents for 1,435
positions.

A more recent tabulation by the Department of
Hospitals, by title rather than occupational group,
reveals a similar picture. This is shown in Table 4.

These listings of existing vacancies do not
tell the entire story of personnel shortages because
the number of budgeted positions, even if all filled,
may be insufficient to provide optimal care. The
following table sums up existing vacancies and estimated additional needs in each category to show how
far the City falls short of providing optimal patient
care in terms of staffing (Table 5).

Were some or all of these positions eventually
put into the Department of Hospitals' budget, vacancies would undoubtedly increase in greater proportion

Table 2

NURSING PERSONNEL POSITIONS, NEW YORK CITY MUNICIPAL HOSPITALS

Title	Authorized Jobs	Vacancies	Filled by Registered Nurses	Filled by Licensed Practical Nurses	Filled by Nurse's Aides	Non-nursing
Superintendent of Nurses	30	1	29			
Assistant Superintendent of Nurses	160	7	153			
Supervisor of Nurses	708	89	619			
Head Nurses and	1,136	209	927			
Head Nurse (Assistant Clinical Instructor)	249	65	184			
Staff Nurses	5,721	662	1,363	930	2,598	168
Total Professional	8,004	1,033	3,275			
Practical Nurses	3,133	150		1,875	1,036	72
Nurse's Aides	5,142	204			4,450	488
Total Nonprofessional	8,275	354		2,805	8,084	728
GRAND TOTAL	16,279	1,387	3,275	2,805	8,084	728

Source: Annual Report of the Department of Hospitals of the City of New York, for the year 1966.

17

Table 3

VACANCIES IN THE MUNICIPAL HOSPITAL SYSTEM
BY MEDICAL OCCUPATIONAL GROUPS, FISCAL 1965

Occupational Group	Budgeted Positions	Number of Employees*	Vacancies
Auxiliary Dental	12	8	4
Bacteriology	235	224	11
Chemistry	139	110	29
Dietician	369	258	111
Health Technician	355	306	49
Laboratory Aide	336	309	27
Medical Service	494	445	49
Pharmacy	119	107	12
Physics	23	14	9
Professional Department Librarian	35	33	2
Psychological	133	111	22
Rehabilitation Therapy	405	254	151
Social Service	459	282	177
TOTAL			653

*Full-time equivalent.

Source: New York City Budget and special computation by Department of Finance.

18

Table 4

VACANCIES IN THE MUNICIPAL HOSPITAL SYSTEM
BY SELECTED OCCUPATIONAL GROUPS, JANUARY 1, 1967

Occupational Title	Budgeted Positions	Number of Employees*	Vacancies
Dietary Aide	2,645	2,541	104
Dietician	246	237	9
Head Dietician	113	109	4
Junior Bacteriologist	124	120	4
Laboratory Aide	307	287	20
Occupational Therapist	90	49	41
Physical Therapist	128	85	43
Social Worker	330	205	125
X-ray Technician	220	183	37
Institutional Aide	2,262	2,113	149
Nurse's Aide	5,474	5,315	159

*Includes provisional employees.

Source: Unpublished data from the files of the New York City Department of Hospitals.

Table 5

ESTIMATED ADDITIONAL PERSONNEL NEEDS TO
PROVIDE OPTIMAL PATIENT CARE, 1967

Category of Personnel	Additional Needs Including Existing Vacancies
Dieticians	212
Food Service Managers	5
Medical Technologists and Technicians	636
Cytotechnologists and Technicians	118
Histologic Technicians	49
Electrocardiograph Technicians	65
Electroencephalograph Technicians	30
Radiologic Technologists and Technicians	312
X-ray Assistants	66
Nuclear Medicine Technologists	25
Nuclear Medicine Assistants	10
Radiation Therapy Technologists and Technicians	9
Laboratory Assistants and Aides	107
Occupational Therapists	157
Occupational Therapy Assistants and Aides	67
Physical Therapists	213
Physical Therapy Assistants and Aides	39
Speech Pathologists and Audiologists	46
Recreation Therapists	75

Inhalation Therapists	77
Licensed Pharmacists	65
Pharmacy Assistants	50
Medical Librarians	18
Medical Record Librarians	64
Medical Record Technicians	60
Social Workers	691
Social Work Assistants and Aides	55
Orthoptic Technicians	4
Surgical Technicians	142
Professional Nurses	2,188
Licensed Practical Nurses	1,096
Nursing Aides, Orderlies, and Attendants	1,986
All Other Professional and Technical Personnel	34
TOTAL	8,781

Source: Robert M. Carr, A Proposal for Training Health Manpower in the City University (Unpublished, November, 1966). Reproduced in Proposal: That a Health Careers Center Be Established in the City University of New York, Draft 3 (Unpublished, March, 1967).

21

than the increase in the number of jobs, for, if
most cannot be staffed now, it would be unrealistic
to expect that adding to demand would alleviate the
problem. This statement, of course, assumes that
relative salaries remain constant and that additional
educational facilities are not developed. The fact
is that a considerable amount of attention in New
York City is being given to health career training
and a lesser amount, but some, to raising the level
of compensation in the municipal system. No doubt
these two approaches will relieve shortages somewhat, particularly in the future, but to do the whole
job, funds in amounts not likely to be forthcoming
would be required.

It is informative to compare the tabulation of
personnel needs in Table 5 with the same computation
for the City's voluntary hospitals, which have about
twice the number of beds. Such a comparison shows
that in only 13 out of 33 categories are the needs
of the voluntary hospitals greater than those of the
municipal institutions. Over-all, the municipal
hospitals need 8,781 additional professional and
technical personnel as against 10,849 for the voluntary hospitals. When the nursing categories are
omitted, the City hospitals' needs are greater--3,511
to 2,433.

The general shortage of skilled health service
personnel, not only in the City but in the nation at
large, can be attributed to relatively recent pressures on demand confronting a virtually static supply
situation. The demand pressures have already been
discussed; the supply situation needs some elucida-
tion. First, financing sources for America's hospitals have always been limited, coming either from
philanthropic or governmental sources. Second, until
recently, trade unions have not been active in the
hospital field, this being a result of the historical
antagonism of governments toward bargaining with their
own employees and of the exclusion of nonprofit organizations from the obligation to engage in collec-
tive bargaining. As a result, wage scales have been
depressed below those available for comparable skills
in the private sector of the economy. Further, before

various kinds of technical employees became important
in the occupational structure, virtually all auxiliary jobs were filled by women, and even today most
are. Because alternative opportunities for females
were relatively rare outside of nursing, teaching,
and social work, their mobility was limited and salaries tended to be somewhat exploitative. With new
and well-paying fields continuing to open up for
women, the low-paying occupations are being increasingly shunned, and vacancies have become more per-
vasive.

Recruitment: Municipal vs. Voluntary Hospitals

The relative disadvantage of the municipal hospitals against other New York City hospitals in at-
tracting personnel can be attributed to four not
necessarily independent factors. First, employment
by municipal governments in the United States has
never been prestigious and continues to have low
priority among graduates of colleges and nursing
schools. This holds true for the New York City government as well.[38] Second, there is a prevailing
view that civil service procedures inhibit ambition
by making merit increases and promotions more dependent on seniority than ability. Third, the hospitals
department procedures are said to inhibit efficiency.
Fourth is the nature of clientele in the municipal
system, the inferior plant, and shortage of technical support.

Wage and salary differentials do not appear to
have been a major cause of the inability of the municipal hospitals to compete successfully with the
voluntary hospitals for whatever professional and
technical personnel are available in the City. Although there is a great deal of variation in the pay
scales of the individual voluntary hospitals, on the
average and with some exceptions, they seem to pay
less for comparable jobs than does the City. This
is shown in Table 6, which compares average weekly
earnings of employees in New York City hospitals
operated by the City and state governments in July,
1966, with those of workers in nongovernmental hospitals in the City. This data is verified by Table 7,

Table 6

AVERAGE STRAIGHT-TIME WEEKLY EARNINGS
FOR SELECTED OCCUPATIONS IN
NEW YORK CITY HOSPITALS,
JULY, 1966

| | Average Weekly Earnings | |
Occupation and Sex	Governmental (Non-Federal)	Non-governmental
Male:		
Medical Social Workers	$141.50	$166.00
Medical Technologists	132.50	109.50
Physical Therapists	123.50	134.00
X-ray Technicians	110.00	110.00
Chief X-ray Technicians	130.50	146.00
Nursing Aides	90.00	72.50
Female:		
Nursing Supervisors	170.00	150.50
Head Nurses	143.00	131.50
General Duty Nurses	127.00	119.50
Dieticians	126.00	123.00
Medical Record Librarians	120.50	151.50
Medical Social Workers	142.50	149.50
Medical Technologists	129.50	113.00
Physical Therapists	125.00	125.50
X-ray Technicians	108.50	111.50
Nursing Aides	91.00	69.00
Practical Nurses (licensed)	97.50	89.00

Source: <u>Earnings and Supplementary Benefits in
Hospitals, New York City</u>, U.S. Department
of Labor, Bureau of Labor Statistics,
July, 1966.

Table 7

ANNUAL BEGINNING SALARIES FOR NEW YORK CITY MUNICIPAL
HOSPITALS AND PRIVATE HOSPITALS IN GREATER NEW YORK, JANUARY 1, 1965

| | ----------- Annual Salary----------- |
Occupation	Private Hospitals (average)	Municipal Hospitals
Head Nurse	$5,865	$6,750
Staff Nurse	5,158	6,050
Practical Nurse	3,952	3,750
Nurse's Aide	3,162	4,000
X-ray Technician	4,618	4,850
Dietician	5,720	5,750
Pharmacist	6,261	6,400
Occupational Therapist	5,762	5,750
Physical Therapist	6,032	5,750

Source: Association of Hospital Personnel Administrators of Greater New York, Wages and Benefits in Hospitals in Greater New York, 1965 Edition; and City of New York Salary Schedules.

which shows annual beginning salaries for a number
of comparable job titles in the City institutions
and in 56 private institutions in greater New York
in 1965. On the assumption that some of the lower-
paying private institutions are in the suburbs, the
wage advantage of the municipal institutions may be
somewhat overstated.

Of course, at any given point of time, one or
another of the systems may have a wage advantage if
general increases have just been received. But in
recent years, after a time lag, the systems have re-
sponded to each other's increases, keeping the long-
run relationship relatively constant. Such has been
the case in the past year. Fifteen of the 37 non-
government hospitals surveyed by the Bureau of Labor
Statistics in July, 1966, granted wage increases between the survey date and December 1, 1966. During
the latter part of 1966, the municipal hospitals also
granted an increase of $375 a year for dietary,
housekeeping, and institutional aides retroactive to
July 1, 1966. Increases for practical nurses, nurse's
aides, and staff nurses were effective January 1,
1967. Some therapists and technicians also received
increases in 1967.

The personnel problem in the City hospitals is
complicated by very large turnover rates in many of
the "shortage" categories. In 1961, the separation
rate for a group of selected City professional, technical, and managerial personnel was 18.4 per cent.
Within the Department of Hospitals, however, only 7
of 16 categories listed in the study had lower rates
than the average. The highest rate of all was 56.2
per cent for staff nurses. These hospitals' occupations and their separation rates are shown in Table
8. Also included is a 1966 computation of separation
rates for some of the same positions and few additional ones.

The forces that act against the equating of
supply and demand in the municipal hospital system
are undoubtedly very powerful ones. No avenue of
attack, whether it be more training facilities, higher salaries, improved personnel procedures, etc.,

Table 8

SEPARATION RATES FOR SELECTED OCCUPATIONS
IN THE NEW YORK CITY HOSPITAL SYSTEM,
1961 AND 1966

| Position | Separation Rate | |
	1961 %	1966 %
Junior Chemist	25.0	n.a.
Dietary Aide	n.a.	16.0
Dietician	21.1	32.0
Head Dietician	n.a.	13.0
Physical Therapist	n.a.	46.0
Occupational Therapist	20.7	67.0
Junior Bacteriologist	11.7	n.a.
Medical Social Worker	18.3	36.0
Junior Psychiatrist	49.5	n.a.
Psychiatrist	14.3	n.a.
Assistant Anaesthesiologist	38.2	n.a.
Anaesthesiologist	14.6	n.a.
Assistant Pathologist	21.3	n.a.
Assistant Roentgenologist	13.3	n.a.
Roentgenologist	13.3	n.a.
Psychologist	18.6	n.a.
Senior Psychologist	15.4	n.a.
X-ray Technician	n.a.	14.0
Institutional Aide	n.a.	29.0
Nurse's Aide	n.a.	27.0
Staff Nurse	56.2	n.a.
Head Nurse	24.7	n.a.

"n.a."--not available.

Source: David T. Stanley et al., Professional
Personnel for the City of New York (Washington, D.C.: Brookings Institution,
1963), 1961 data, pp. 30-33; 1966 data
from 1967 Department of Personnel Survey
of Manpower Needs.

can be overlooked. Nevertheless, the supply-demand
imbalance is of such magnitude that there is some
question whether approaches aimed at increasing supply can be successful enough to correct it. Working
on this premise, a large number of writers have suggested that more attention needs to be paid to the
quality and utilization of existing manpower. It is
this alternative, the "new careers" concept, to which
we turn in Chapter 2.

NOTES

1. U.S. Department of Health, Education, and
Welfare, Social Security Administration, Social
Security Bulletin, Vol. 28, No. 10 (October, 1965),
p. 10.

2. U.S. Department of Labor, Bureau of Labor
Statistics, "Health, Manpower Trends" (Mimeograph,
March, 1967), p. 17.

3. Gerald J. Boyle, "Projection of New York
City Expenditures to 1975," in Financing Government
in New York City (Graduate School of Public Administration, New York University, 1966), pp. 249-83.

4. Katherine W. Strauss, "Financing Major
Social Services, ibid., pp. 347-98.

5. City of New York, Executive Capital Budget
for 1967-68, p. x.

6. Alonzo S. Yerby at Conference on Health
Care in the Cities, Barnard College, April 1, 1967.

7. The New York Times, May 5, 1967.

8. Ibid., May 8, 1967.

9. Ibid., May 6, 1967.

10. Ibid., editorial, May 9, 1967.

11.   Dr. Martin Cherkasky at Conference on Health Care in the Cities.

12.   The New York Times, March 16, 1967.

13.   Interview with Dr. Ray E. Trussell, March 15, 1967.

14.   The New York Times, May 11, 1967. However, 13 new contracts negotiated in May, 1967, provide for closer supervision over physicians and equipment and a reduction in administrative costs (The New York Times, May 16, 1967).

15.   Professor Frank Van Dyke of the Columbia University School of Public Health at Conference on Health Care in the Cities.

16.   Conference on Health Care in the Cities.

17.   Interview with Dr. Ray E. Trussell, March 15, 1967.

18.   Interview with Health Services Administrator Brown, March 13, 1967.

19.   The New York Times, February 12, March 24, and May 5, 1967.

20.   National Commission on Community Health Services, Health is a Community Affair (Cambridge, Mass.: Harvard University Press, 1966), p. 19.

21.   City of New York, Executive Capital Budget for 1967-68, p. x.

22.   Ibid.

23.   Recommendations of the Institute for Policy Studies reported in The New York Times, May 11, 1967.

24.   The New York Times, May 8, 1967, and interview with Health Services Administrator Brown, March 13, 1967.

25. Herman M. Sturm, "Technological Developments and Their Effects Upon Health Manpower," _Monthly Labor Review_, January, 1967, p. 4.

26. Ibid., p. 5.

27. _Manpower Resources in Hospitals, 1966_, Summary Report of a Survey conducted by the Bureau of Health Manpower, Public Health Service, Department of Health, Education, and Welfare and the American Hospital Association, June, 1967, p. 3.

28. William Mirengoff, "Health Manpower--An Emerging Challenge," _Employment Service Review_, November, 1966, p. 8.

29. National Commission on Community Health Services, _op. cit._, p. 81.

30. _The New York Times_, February 15, 1967.

31. Interview with Health Services Administrator Brown, March 13, 1967.

32. _The New York Times_, April 6, 1967.

33. _Ibid._, October 6, 1966.

34. _Ibid._, April 6, 1967.

35. _Ibid._, October 6, 1966.

36. _Ibid._, April 4, 1967.

37. _Ibid._, March 8, 1967.

38. David T. Stanley _et al._, _Professional Personnel for the City of New York_ (Washington, D.C.: The Brookings Institution, 1963), pp. 64-67.

CHAPTER **2** THE "NEW CAREERS" CONCEPT
AND ITS APPLICABILITY TO
HEALTH SERVICES

The passage of the Economic Opportunity Act in
1964 was the signal for the re-emergence of the concept of job redesign, usually defined as the removal
of nonprofessional tasks from professional and technical jobs in order to create new and simplified occupations that can be performed by relatively unskilled persons. The idea was not new; it had been
in scattered use for at least 30 years, especially
during World War II, when critical shortages of
skilled manpower led to the discovery that intelli-
gence, ability, and problem-solving capacity could
be found at all levels of society. As a result, entrance qualifications were eased, on-the-job training
programs instituted, and jobs redesigned to fit the
job to the worker. The same approach was and still
is taken by the armed forces, which trains nonprofessionals to perform what are usually considered professional tasks. This is particularly the case with
respect to the provision of medical and educational
services.

In the 1950's, generally characterized by a
slack labor market, the credential-centered society
reasserted itself. Academic degrees, licenses, years
of experience again became the accepted predictors
of potential job performance. But several socio-
economic counterforces were at work that would crys-
tallize with the passage of the Economic Opportunity
Act. These were the rapid postwar growth of the
public sector, a general shortage of professionals
within it, and relatively high levels of unemployment, particularly among minority groups.

With the creation of the Community Action programs under the Office of Economic Opportunity (OEO),
Congress declared that there should be "maximum feasible participation" of the poor in all parts of the
program, including staffing. This mandate, which itself arose from a growing recognition of the poten-
tially constructive contributions of the poor, resulted in the employment of between 40,000 and 50,000
nonprofessionals as aides to teachers, social workers,
and others.[1] Unfortunately, these jobs have generally had only one entry level, salaries have been barely
above poverty level, and training has been limited
and piecemeal.

Nevertheless, there has been a demonstration
effect. The idea has spread outside the antipoverty
programs to governmental institutions such as hospitals, schools, and welfare agencies to the Federal
Civil Service and even to some private businesses.
The concept was formalized and given its widely used
title in the work New Careers for the Poor.[2] Most
recently, it was granted Congressional recognition
by the passage of the Scheuer-Nelson amendments to
the Economic Act of 1966. "New careers" is, of
course, not the only name by which the concept is
known. Others are job redesign, restructuring, and
creation of intermediate-level jobs. The "new careerist" also answers to the name nonprofessional, subprofessional, and paraprofessional.

In brief, the major goal of the proposal is
the provision of a sufficient number of employment
opportunities for all unemployed persons, with particular emphasis on the needs of the uneducated and
unskilled. In addition, the jobs must be permanent,
of clear social utility, and have a place on a
"career ladder." Education and training opportunities must be a part of the career scheme and be
available at the work place or in nearby community
institutions at no cost to the worker. Under such
a set-up, there need be no limitation, short of basic
ability and ambition, on movement to the very top of
the "job ladder." The latter point is of utmost importance. As Pearl and Riessman put it, "The relationship of work and education must be recast so that
the two become overlapping."[3]

The situation that has historically prevailed
in hospitals must thus be avoided. There, nonprofessionals such as nurse's aides have been used for
many years, but there have been few if any opportunities available to them for training and promotions.
Under a "new careers" program, "It would be possible
for a person to enter as a hospital aide (involving
primarily unskilled tasks); graduate to a nurse's
aide (which would involve somewhat more responsible
work); move upward to practical nurse (with a more
demanding but supervised relationship with patients);
and ultimately move on to ever increasing challenges
and responsibilities as a registered nurse."[4]

The method by which these goals can be accomplished is "to remove from the jobs of professionals
all of the tasks that do not truly require professional skill; hierarchize those tasks at ascending
levels of responsibility; hire the non-professional
and train him at the work site to do his job and
then to move him up to the next level."[5] In some
cases, particularly in the human-service area, there
are new tasks for the nonprofessional in addition to
those taken out of the professional's hands. These
"relate to the potential of the non-professional to
function as a peer" with the poor "and in a more
subjective fashion."[6]

Although Pearl, Riessman, and others stress
the goal of training and employing the unemployed
poor, it should be pointed out that the approach has
benefits for employers as well. Not only does it
help relieve shortages of professional and technical
personnel, but it should reduce the labor cost of
every particular unit of work since it assigns each
unit to the least skilled worker capable of doing
it.

What is impressive about the "new careers" concept is its pinpointing of the dynamic relationships
among poverty, education, and employment opportunities. Its approach is nothing less than a total
attack on all psychological and sociological barriers
and on all institutional arrangements that prevent
the deprived groups in society, particularly the
motivated and talented among them, from advancing to

"any station available to the more favored members
of the society."[7]

The approach does not simply attempt to remedy
income levels; rather, it provides meaningful career
opportunities to the poor and, by doing so, helps
overcome the problem of lack of motivation, aliena-
tion from work, and other poverty-related problems
connected with the fact that deadend jobs are the
principal opportunities for the unskilled poor.

Another important policy stresses the continuous availability of training opportunities. The individual is hired "as is" and put to work at a level
appropriate to his ability and allowed to move on as
ready. The key to his advancement is systematic
training both in the field and in courses in technical institutes or in community colleges designed to
meet the needs of the "new careerist" on his way up
the job ladder. Thus, these courses must be related
to the problems and experiences encountered on the
job. Institutions of higher education are challenged
to make themselves "more relevant, more critical,
more closely related to reality."[8] And it must be
fully appreciated that "there can be no end to poverty" unless "for the most part, training for the
poor . . . take(s) place _after_ employment is secured."[9]
This means both formal and on-the-job training. Although credentials and degrees may still be requisites
to advancement, the newly created training programs
must be accepted as alternative ways to acquire credentials. Thus, in addition to the normal high
school-college-professional school route, there will
exist others that dropouts from the formal process
can use to advance themselves. This requires, in
addition to the development of new education and
training schemes, the cooperation of professional accreditation and licensing bodies who must first accept
the "new careers" concept and then relate it to their
traditional standards.

Further, the new jobs must be permanent ones
and therefore must become a part of the organizational
structure. They must not be marginal or make-work
jobs forever supported by antipoverty grants. In the

case of government, therefore, they must be "legiti-
mized" by becoming part of the civil service structure.

To the extent that certain public institutions
are "colonial impositions" in that they operate for
the poor as clients but without their collaboration,
the "new careers" concept provides a corrective. It
involves the poor in programs that affect them. In
some cases, they help develop policy; in almost all
cases, they maintain personal contact with users of
the service. By doing so, they act as a bridge between the isolated poor and the larger middle-class
society.

Finally, in answer to the question of how many
public service jobs can be created, Pearl and
Riessman answer that "in an affluent automated society, the number of persons needed . . . equals the
number of persons for whom there are no other jobs."[10]
The reasoning is based on the premise that virtually
all public services are under-financed and that the
entire society benefits from "adequate health, education, welfare and recreation." Short of reaching the
level of adequacy, no expenditure can be considered
wasteful. In this context, we undoubtedly have something to learn from planned economies. Emily Clark
Brown, Professor Emeritus at Vassar, pointed out recently that "the U.S.S.R. Council of Ministers put
responsibility directly on Government and party au-
thorities from republic levels down to every region,
city and local district to assure opportunity for
education or jobs for all school graduates or school
leavers." This means expansion of technical and
university facilities and the creation of new jobs
with training. Enterprises are assigned quotas
ranging from .5 per cent to 10 per cent of their work
force depending on the possibilities of absorption.[11]

Institutional arrangements vary from one country to another, but the example helps us to remember
that from the standpoint of economy as a whole, additional national product created by the previously
unemployed is "costless" in that it involves no opportunity cost or sacrifice of alternative goods and
services.

That the "new careers" concept is applicable
to the health services industry has been pointed out
by numerous studies of its occupational structure.
Hospitals particularly are characterized by sharp
demarcations between the professional and nonprofessional with licenses, degrees, and professional association accreditations attesting to the gulf. The
relationship of all groups of workers to each other
as part of a "team" is obscured by a craft-union approach wherein particular tasks are made the property
of a group and guarded against raiding by rival guilds.

Nevertheless, there have in recent years been
significant attempts to improve the utilization and
organization of hospital manpower to overcome shortages and increase efficiency. Not all this activity
was the result of conscious policy; rather, some took
the form of the diversification of health occupations
under the impact of changing treatment and technology.
The new occupations, such as medical technologists,
medical record librarians, and physical and occupational therapists, have shown the greatest rate of
growth between 1950 and 1960. Today, only one of
five health workers are physicians, as contrasted to
three of five in 1900. In general, since the turn of
the century, jobs with the "lowest level of job content" have had the highest growth rate, whereas those
with the "highest levels" have shown the smallest
increases.[12]

Other changes and attempts at changes have been
made as the direct result of the realization or sus-
picion that many employees spend a substantial amount
of their time performing duties far below their levels
of capacity.

THE VA EXPERIENCES

The Veteran's Administration (VA) for a number
of years has encouraged its hospitals to study the
utilization of nursing service personnel and has developed methodology to assist them. It places emphasis on the questions of whether particular duties
"need to be done" and "by whom they may be done most

appropriately."[13]   Developed from an earlier study,
"Utilization of Nursing Service Personnel," and
carried out at the Veteran's Administration Hospital
in The Bronx, New York, in 1957, the VA Guide outlines in depth the necessary procedures for implementing studies of nursing utilization.   The basic
framework provides for individual recording of work
activities at five-minute intervals.   The accumulated
job tasks are then judged by several committees as
to their appropriateness as nursing functions.

        The application and use of this technique in
the nursing service has received wide support from
various VA hospitals.   Results have clearly shown
what nursing supervisors had continually alleged--
that the nursing function had become quite vague,
with a multitude of nonnursing duties being performed
by the nursing staff.   As the nursing personnel are
continually on duty twenty-four hours a day, "the
nurse and her helpers have found themselves acting in
the capacities of housekeepers, repairmen, plumbers,
clerks, laboratory, pharmacy, and food-service workers, etc."[14]   As the additional tasks were performed
by nursing personnel over a period of time, they came
to be identified as rightful duties of the nursing
function, paid for from the nursing budget.

        One of a number of examples is the study im-
plemented by the VA hospital in Grand Junction, Colorado.   In 1961, a job-activity log survey was exe-
cuted over a two-day period.   The purpose of the
study was to isolate both quantitative and qualitative information along the following lines:

        (1) Who was performing the activities?

        (2) What activities were performed by various
            levels of nursing?

        (3) When and where were these activities
            being performed?

        The study established that 49 per cent of the
recorded activities were appropriate to the skills of
the nursing staff.   Also, of total time measured, 53

per cent was spent by all staff personnel on direct
and indirect nursing activities. However, it was
noted that the nursing aides and assistants were
providing a higher percentage of patient care than
the professional nurses.[15] The obvious recommendation from this survey was for a removal of the nursing personnel from performing all housekeeping,
dietary, clerical, and laundry duties and to return
them to activities more in line with their skills
and training.

A follow-up study was conducted one year later
to evaluate any changes in the allocation of nursing
personnel time. These changes are shown below:

	July 9&10 1961	September 9&10 1962
	(Percentages of Daily Shift spent at this activity)	
Activity		
(1) Direct Nursing Care		
Head Nurses	16.5	28.1
Staff Nurses	40.5	37.6
Nursing Assistants	44.9	49.7
(2) Indirect Nursing Care		
Head Nurses	24.0	34.9
Staff Nurses	30.5	35.6
Nursing Assistants	9.8	10.9

The over-all results show that time spent on
direct and indirect nursing care increased across
the board with one exception. Also, there were de-
creases in time spent on both clerical and dietary
activities, again indicating improved utilization
of personnel.[16]

A more recent study was done in the VA hospital in Dearborn, Michigan. As a first step in job
breakdown, eighty-eight separate activities were
listed for coding. An evaluation jury then graded
28 per cent of the activities as "appropriate," 18
per cent as "inappropriate," and 52 per cent "ques-
tionable."[17] The inference here was that while 18

per cent of the job tasks were obviously out of
place, at least 50 per cent of the duties were un-
assignable. This was the case because, for many
tasks, the particular situation is the important determinant of whether an activity is appropriate or
not. Thus, one sees an immediate difficulty in restructuring; i.e., what does one do with activities
that cannot be strictly assigned to one specific job?

In spite of the difficulty of assigning all
job activities, the study was still able to show that
only 53 per cent of the nursing personnel's time was
spent in direct and indirect nursing care. This figure is similar to the one for the Grand Junction survey. The Dearborn study also showed that neither
teaching nor supervision was receiving enough time
from the nursing staffs. Finally, this study gave
positive supportive evidence to the view of nursing
personnel that their relationship with patients was
eroding. Nonprofessional personnel were found to
average 10 per cent more time in "Direct Nursing
Care" than the professional nurse.[18]

The conclusion of the study demonstrated the
need for realignment of job activities and functions.
The study committee felt the contention of misutili-
zation voiced by the nursing administration had been
completely justified:

> If a professional nurse is tied to desk
> duties that keep her out of the patient
> area, she is not going to know when non-
> professional personnel need guidance and
> supervision, nor is she going to be able
> to develop the staff; she is not going to
> be there when the patient and/or his fam-
> ily are at a readiness point to learn
> principles that will help him to maintain
> health and be able to live usefully out-
> side of the hospital; she will not be able
> to be where she belongs--in the patient
> unit--available for help and advice and
> support. If a nursing assistant has to
> hurry through his patient care duties in
> time to pass and collect trays . . . he

is not performing at his highest capacity nor performing the duties for which
he was hired and trained and paid.[19]

Recommendations derived from this study covered primarily institutional and technical services that had
claimed roughly 26 per cent of the nursing staff's
time. The activity analysis showed that these supplementary services were not properly administered,
and nursing personnel were forced to perform these
functions. As a result, these service departments
were asked to: (1) provide more of their own personnel; (2) organize supply stocks for the various
wards and to maintain constant levels; and (3) allo-
cate department members to work evening and weekend
shifts.

The emphasis of these suggestions should be
apparent. Additional housekeeping employees are
needed to maintain cleanliness in the wards, previously performed by nurses. Clerical people are
required to take over "charting" and similar work
from the nursing personnel. Also, more clerks are
needed for charting and administrative duties on
evening shifts. The technical services need to better organize medical supplies and drugs in the wards
so that the nurses will not have to be added to the
wards to relieve the nursing staff of the necessity
of carrying X-rays to clinic, picking up laboratory
slips, taking specimens to the laboratory, etc.

The recommended changes exemplify the nursing
dilemma. Where supporting staffs have lacked resources, they have surrendered their functions to
nursing personnel. In some cases, this has been
formalized to the point of developing new job classifications. Rhoda Russell, Dean of the School of
Nursing and Director of the Nursing Service of the
University of Michigan, expressed the problem suc-
cinctly in the following manner: "Nurses need to
be serviced in their professional functions, rather
than servicing all others. . . . We need to look at
. . . and plan (how) to give the patient back to the
nurse and not to others."[20]

The two VA examples are important for several
reasons. First, they have demonstrated a methodology which, within limits, is able to classify job
tasks. Next, they have been able to show the changing nature of jobs and job functions within the hospital system. Third, while the interest of these
nursing services has not been on creating new job
packages nor job careers, the examples have pointed
out the feasibility of explicitly attacking a job
structure with the purpose of realigning job activities.

THE NEW YORK CITY EXPERIENCES

In the New York metropolitan area, health and
educational personnel have continually been leaders
in developing new conceptual approaches to the efficient utilization of medical resources. For example,
in the early 1950's, studies of nursing personnel
utilization in the municipal hospital system were
conducted by New York University graduate students.
The previously cited VA Guide was developed in the
Bronx in 1957. More currently, various hospitals
are experimenting with unit managers, obstetric
technicians, social worker aides, etc. New technology is being considered as a method of relieving the
professional staffs of clerical, housekeeping, and
maintenance tasks. New training programs to provide
increased degrees of job responsibility and opportunity are being developed for professional health
employees in the City.

RESTRUCTURING--THE PUBLIC HEALTH TEAM

Recently, the New York City Department of
Health initiated a study program to measure nursing
personnel utilization in their Public School Visiting
Program. The study was undertaken because of the
continuous loss of full-time public health nurses
over a twelve-year period. The Department had 735
full-time nurses in 1953, and the number was reduced
to 335 by 1965. However, the Health Department in

the same period created a nonprofessional position
entitled Public Health Assistant (PHA). This job
category, in conjunction with staff nurses and part-
time nurses, was used to fill the vacancies left by
the Public Health Nurse. The PHA soon came to play
a large role in the health program as numbers increased from 57 initially to 466 in 1965.[21] But,
even this implementation of a new job classification
was insufficient for health needs; the Department of
Health estimated in 1965 that it was unable to reach
118,000 students in 83 public and parochial schools
because of the continued nurse shortage. As a result, the Department concluded that it needed to investigate other methods of alleviating the problem.

Thus, a study was undertaken to investigate
the possibility of using the existing supply of nursing personnel more effectively.

The methodology of the study was based on the
VA outline. Doctors, nurses, and PHAs kept daily
logs of all work performed. From a total of 1,000
schools, a sample of 335 elementary and junior high
schools were selected; this allowed a total of 3,189
activity logs to be coded. Based on this sampling
procedure, it was estimated from the log activity
analysis that, out of 373,000 hours spent by nurses
in elementary and junior high school programs, more
than one third (125,000 hours) were used for work
below the level of professional nursing skills. Public Health personnel commenting on the findings
stated, "This study shows that if we could organize
so that our nurses took the time they spend now on
some subprofessional activities and turned to professional activities, we would be achieving the same
result as if we had more nurses on staff."[22]

To test possible new approaches to better personnel utilization, the Department of Public Health
organized a demonstration project. The school health
team was reconstructed so that there was a "public
health nurse team leader who would carry a carefully
selected caseload, serve as a community nurse in the
team's geographical area and generally advise the
other team members on the public health nursing

approach to their caseload."[23] She would review all
records of home visits and would distribute those
home visits which the staff nurse could handle.

Each experimental health team consisted of a
public health nurse, a staff nurse, a doctor, and
a public health assistant. Each doctor who formerly
visited schools on a random basis now was assigned
to a specific area. This allowed him to be specifically cognizant of particular problems in his area
and to be able to maintain continual checks on his
patients. As the public health nurse was given the
responsibility of team leader and coordinator, most
of her "nonnursing" duties were delegated to the
public health assistant. The PHA now worked more
closely with the doctor. She maintained all child
health records, "screening" children who should be
referred to the public health nurse, assisting in
immunizations and examinations, etc. Finally, as
the new health team was able to become "case ori-
ented," they held meetings as required to discuss
particular needs of their area.

This approach to better manpower utilization
appears to have worked out quite successfully. Early
indications show that a majority of the teams have
been very pleased with the "restructuring" of work.
The doctors report greater satisfaction and enthusiasm from being able to identify with specific schools
and their individual problems. The PHAs have become
full members of the health team and have indicated
real enjoyment from a "closer relationship to the
professional side of the work." The actual casework
within the communities has become better organized
and priorities more easily pinpointed. Finally, the
expenditure of nursing time has been highly improved
by "the utilization of each member at his highest
level."

NURSE: MIDWIFE IN COMMUNITY HOSPITALS

Among the more important health needs in New
York City is improved maternity care. Good maternity
care presupposes prenatal medical attention; yet,

in Manhattan "about half the pregnant women go through
their pregnancies with insufficient care--if they receive any at all. Moreover, the number of Manhattan
women who go through pregnancy and birth unseen by
a doctor continues to increase."[24] The major defi-
ciency presently preventing good maternity care is
the lack of medically trained personnel.

This problem has several aspects. First, ob-
stetricians are in limited supply. Second, they are
highly concentrated in the upper middle-class suburbs. This intensifies the shortages in critical
slum areas with their higher birth rates.

One solution now being implemented by Dr. Louis
Hellman at Kings County Hospital is increased use of
the nurse-midwife. Although not a new approach--80
per cent of the world's babies are delivered by mid-
wives--it is relatively rare in the United States.
It is significant that the eleven countries with
lower infant mortalities than the United States all
employ midwives.

Close to 100 nurse-midwives have been trained
over an eight-year period by the obstetrics staff at
Kings County, and their over-all success, according
to Dr. Hellman, has been excellent. With a background of licensed nursing and special midwifery
training, the nurse-midwife acts as the chief assistant to a ward obstetrician in the hospital. Where
a birth is considered normal, the nurse-midwife is
in complete charge. "She sees her patients throughout pregnancy and labor. She delivers the child,
administers drugs when they are needed during labor
and delivery and later she visits the patient after
the birth and conducts the usual six weeks postpartum examination."[25]

Patients who have been questioned about care
received from the nurse-midwife tend to be quite
enthusiastic. This reaction is derived from the
fact that she usually takes a greater personal interest in the patient than the overworked doctor
who normally cannot spare more than a few minutes
for each patient. At the same time, the doctor's

time can now be better utilized, as he need only be
in attendance for those births expected to present
"complications."

There are several reasons behind nurse-midwife
acceptance in hospital obstetrics. First, there is
a recognition that the highly trained and experienced
resident obstetrician need not occupy himself with
routine, normal deliveries. Numerous doctors honest-
ly admit that Americans are excessively demanding in
insisting on all medical attention from a "medical
doctor." Thus, since a real shortage of maternity
personnel exists, the nurse-midwife is finding her
role readily received.

A second and equally important factor is the
direct contact the midwife has with the patient.
Ideally, contact should begin with patients during
the prenatal period so that the nurse-midwife can
advise on dietary needs, forms of exercise, expectant
labor symptoms, etc. This type of personal relationship becomes especially important to the poor and
illiterate, those heavily represented in the minority
groups who utilize the municipal hospitals. It is
among this group that complications and abnormally
high rates of premature births occur. Also, as a
lack of communication and fear of inattention is
present, these patients need care in addition to that
now available in the hospital system. In this context, the properly trained nurse-midwife can play
a very important role. By her continual contact with
patients, she is able to alleviate fears. After
birth is accomplished, her presence may induce the
patient to return for postnatal checkups and thus
enter a new phase of actual understanding and attention to personal health. In this manner, the nurse-
midwife plays a dual role--medical competence combined with social awareness.

Similar to previous examples, the nurse-midwife
represents only a piecemeal approach to restructuring.
As a real shortage in medical personnel was apparent,
specific steps were taken to correct it. No application of the "new careers" concept was attempted.
However, it is important to note that nurse-midwife

job classification demonstrates that, where a need
is present, it is possible to shift certain job activities to less-trained members of the medical staff.
Thus, the obstetrician finds some of his duties now
being reassigned with no loss in the quality of over-
all care.

THE NURSE AT LOEB CENTER

The Loeb Center for Nursing and Rehabilitation,
located at Montefiore Hospital, has now been in operation for four years under the direction of Lydia
T. Hall. The center operates, as the director points
out, as an intermediary between "the acute general
hospital and the home." It is distinguished from a
hospital-type institution in that emphasis is on
nursing care as distinguished from medical care.
Nursing care is defined not as a group of separable
physical activities; rather, the nurse combines her
medical knowledge with nurturing, counseling, and
teaching. Mrs. Hall explains it in this way: "Here,
the nurse is a 'carer,' a nurturer. She works with
the patient constantly to get him back on his feet,
to help him understand his illness. The patient
learns and the learning process help him to heal."

As an approach to improved medical care, Loeb
Center emphasizes the need to unify the nursing activities. The proposition is put forth that unifi-
cation is the distinctive mark of quality nursing.
Loeb Center makes no use of practical nurses or
nursing aides. It is felt that it is "the professional nurse, with her background in biological,
physical and social sciences, who is most able to
give intimate bodily care. . . . Whatever is done
directly with the patient is done by the professional
nurse."[26]

Implicit in this approach is a restructuring
of job duties on an ascending scale. Contrary to
delegating more activities to other personnel, the
nurse receives additional duties, those most relevant to direct patient care. However, the nurse at
Loeb Center does not claim to replace the hospital

nurse. They have different functions, with the Loeb
nurse having a specialized job of rehabilitation.

One of the more interesting aspects of Loeb
Center has been the over-all reaction by nurses,
doctors, and patients. The Center is probably one
of few nursing institutions that have a continual
waiting line for employment. Nurses come because
they say they want to practice nursing rather than
to administrate, coordinate, and supervise other
groups. Doctors also have had favorable comments to
make about the Center. A survey taken among a group
of doctors 14 months after the Center opened provided
the following information:

(1) A random sample of 40 respondents on
the quality of nursing at Loeb gave 1
good, 38 excellent, and 1 superb.

(2) The sample of doctors stated that Loeb
shortened the hospitalization of their
patients by an average of three weeks.

Finally, remarks from patients have indicated a real
enthusiasm for this intensive nursing care. They
have enjoyed the freedom and personal attention provided by the Center.

The Center maintains a high nurse-patient
ratio of one to eight, which is a remarkable contrast to the situation in some municipal hospitals
of one professional nurse per 100 patients. However, Mrs. Hall points out that the difference in
nurse-patient ratios does not tell the whole story.
Because hospitalization is cut down through intensive care, less hospital beds need to be maintained.
This implies that part of the shortage in nursing
personnel is the result of poor care; i.e., patients
stay longer, occupy more beds, and amplify the necessary patient-nurse ratio. Also, cost comparisons
are quite favorable for the Center. Montefiore Hospital charges an average of $60 per day for patient
maintenance. At Loeb Center, operating at capacity,
costs have been calculated between $19 and $30 per
day.[27]

Loeb Center provides another example of the restructuring of an accepted and traditional job category. As was mentioned earlier, the nursing role is
enlarged, not subdivided. However, this was done
because it was felt that quality rehabilitation de-
manded this type of specialization handled only by a
highly trained staff. But, more significantly, Mrs.
Hall is suggesting that there are at least several
types of nurses; thus, in place of our standard form
of nursing, taught in the various nursing schools,
one may be able to define a variety of professions:
rehabilitation, clinical work, general hospital care,
teaching, administration, technicians, laboratory,
etc.

LINCOLN HOSPITAL: NONPROFESSIONAL JOBS

Lincoln Hospital in the South Bronx has been a
leader in the utilization of nonprofessional workers
to fill manpower shortages in the medical field. The
initial emphasis was to relieve the critical shortage
of RN's in the various wards. Second, Lincoln Hospital was interested in establishing greater participation of the South Bronx community in ameliorating
their own health deficiencies. Also, as high unemployment has been critical in this area, the creation
of additional nonprofessional jobs would provide some
badly needed work in the community.

The basic approach in job redesign has been
generally similar to the previously mentioned examples. In the place of a formal evaluation of job
tasks, Lincoln Hospital has relied on a more informal methodology. A number of nonprofessional jobs
have been created, and, in each case, the senior
staff people have decided which activities could and
should be restructured. Also, it has been left to
the department heads to establish and operate their
own individual training programs. Thus, in contrast
to the reallocation of job activities within a given
occupational structure, Lincoln Hospital has brought
in a number of new employees. The result has been
improved care with broader career possibilities for
low-income employees.

The first of the nonprofessional restructured
jobs was developed by Dr. Joseph Smith, Chief of Obstetrics. Because of the great demands on nursing personnel in the maternity wards plus continued inadequate staffing, it was decided to develop an obstetrics (OB) technician. Specifically, the OB technician is an assistant who works with the doctor in the
delivery room when nurses are not available. In contrast to the nurse-midwife, who performs the actual
delivery, the OB technician has duties such as check-
ing the fetal heart beat and taking the mother's
blood pressure. In addition, she stays with the patients before, throughout, and after delivery, giving
personal attention not previously available because
of personnel shortages. As the program has taken
shape, the OB technician is being trained so that she
may absorb up to 50 per cent of the activities presently performed by registered nurses. Joseph V.
Terenzio, Commissioner of Hospitals, has remarked
that Dr. Smith now maintains one of the better OB
clinics in the municipal hospital system. Also,
other hospitals are sending personnel to Lincoln to
be trained as OB technicians.

A second type of job restructuring now func-
tioning at Lincoln Hospital is in the clerical field.
Nurses throughout the United States have remarked
about the excessive and growing clerical work they
must handle. In response, various types of administrative positions have been developed to remove these
duties from the nursing staff. At Lincoln, three
such positions have been designated: the Unit Manager, the Chart-Care Technician, and the Ward Manager.

The Unit Manager acts as an administrative assistant in the medical clinic. Many clerical and
recording duties are his. He is responsible for
maintaining supply levels and performing other related work. At present, four unit managers (one for
each clinic) are at Lincoln. This allows the nursing staff to spend additional time with patients.

The second clerical position, Chart-Care Technician, is used in the Pediatrics (child care) Clinic.
This job was developed to be performed by members

of the Job Corps. The duties are the "charting" of
patient progress and other records normally maintained by nurses. These activities include recording patient temperatures, pulse rates, blood pressure, number of visits, sickness symptoms, etc. All
the clerical-type recordings become the responsibility of the Chart-Care Technician. In this manner,
more time is available to the professional staff.

The Ward Manager, similar to the Unit Manager,
was created to take over clerical and related activities of the registered nurse in the various hospital
wards. They keep supplies at adequate levels and are
responsible for maintaining ward upkeep and for coordinating housekeeping activities. At Lincoln, the
Ward Manager position was initiated slowly. The hospital administration first hired a recent college
graduate who was given the task of learning all of
the nonnursing activities selected for the Ward Manager. At the end of a six-month period, she took on
the responsibility of developing and supervising a
training program for Ward Managers.

The new jobs described above have worked well
at Lincoln. As a result, a number of additional
nonprofessional jobs are being considered. A Medical
Technician, who would work directly with doctors in
a position similar to that of an Army corpsman, is
being discussed. Also, Federal funds are currently
available to train Mental Health Aides, who would
work in the psychiatric wards.

In conjunction with several satellite health
centers which Lincoln has established in the South
Bronx Community under the HELP Program, a number of
"aide" positions are being studied. These are:

(1) Social Aide
(2) Home Economics Aide
(3) Medical Aide
(4) Maternity Aide
(5) Dental Aide

These nonprofessional aide positions are not
directly linked to on-premise hospital work; however,

the staff at Lincoln Hospital feels that hospital
facilities need to be extended into the community.
For example, Dr. Smith points out that the high (20
per cent) premature birth rate among Lincoln patients
is primarily a reflection of the social conditions
of the South Bronx Community. In this manner, he
sees the "social pathology" of the community as the
cause of many treatable illnesses and diseases.

Hospital patients are said to need a continuity
of medical care--care that occurs before coming to
the hospital and after hospitalization has been end-
ed. Thus, the hospital has the duty to involve itself
in the community, from which a great number of the
health problems originate.

Concurrent with these beginnings in job restructuring through the employment and training of
"nonprofessional" people, the Albert Einstein College
of Medicine--the voluntary affiliate Lincoln Hospi-
tal--is developing a "new careers" training program.
Recently, a preliminary proposal has been submitted
and accepted by the Human Resources Administration
for a $50,000 grant to initiate a trial program. The
main emphasis is to establish "a series of career
tracks" accessible to nonprofessional employees. A
summary of the goals the program hopes to accomplish
are as follows:

a. Provision of needed health manpower.

b. Education for the subprofessional, lead-
    ing to full job competence and qualifying
    certification.

c. Opportunity for the preprofessional to
    further pursue a career leading to full
    professional status.

d. Development of a sense of community
    commitment and stimulation of potential
    community participation in health services.[28]

The restructuring and current training program
represent one of the better developed schemes for

implementing the "new careers" concept. It started
in a similar manner as the earlier mentioned programs,
nurse-wife, Public Health Assistant, etc. Each of
the new positions was developed to fulfill a specific
need. Except by obtaining outside education and
training, all of these jobs have held little prospect
for advancement. However, as the second step, the
Albert Einstein Medical College Training program has
as its goal the development of vertically ascending
careers. Although the program is only in its early
stages, its appearance demonstrates a significant
movement from the potential idea of "new careers" into an ongoing program.

     At Lincoln, there has been no significant re-
sistance to the training of nonprofessional workers
to perform duties formerly delegated to the professional staff. This may well be a function of the
nature of the community surrounding the hospital.
Here one finds a high index of poverty, crime, and
unemployment. Consequently, nursing and other medical personnel are difficult to attract to this neighborhood, and opposition to nonprofessional training
programs is minimized. Critics voice a concern for
a deterioration of quality, but Lincoln Hospital
administrators feel that, if anything, the quality
of care has improved. However, one question remains
very real. If the environmental conditions present
at Lincoln did not exist, would the program be as
widely accepted both among professionals and among
patients of wider experience and education?

               GOUVERNEUR HOSPITAL: SOCIAL WORKER AIDE

     The need to build a stronger bridge between
the hospital and the community it serves is the main
focus of a social worker aide training program now
under way at Gouverneur Hospital on the Lower East
Side of Manhattan. As does Dr. Smith at Lincoln,
Gouverneur Hospital Administrator Harold Light has
stressed the need to put trained people into the
communities in order to reach residents before they
become hospital patients. Specifically, there is
a need to improve communication between low-income
neighborhoods and their community medical centers.

Shortages of medical personnel in all fields
has resulted in the appearance of gaps in over-all
community health programs. This situation is what
many doctors and medical personnel refer to as "frag-
mented medicine" or "discontinuity" in medical care.
At Gouverneur, there was found to be a lack of effective communication between medical personnel and
social workers and between social workers and the
community.

As a result, Manpower Development Training Act
funds have been obtained for the training of indigenous personnel to act as social worker aides within
the local community. Ths initial program indicates
that community interest is high. When Gouverneur
Hospital issued a request for applicants to 60 positions, it received 700 applications!

The social worker aide is to have an important
role. Being a member of the community in which he
will work, a reasonable knowledge of community problems will be available to him, and he is expected to
have a very personal interest in the people of his
neighborhood. His position of working with the professional social worker gives him a dual responsibility: (1) to act as a liaison between the community and the social worker, and (2) to obtain skills
through association, training, etc., with the social
worker.

Mr. Light points out that the professional social worker has encountered an identification crisis.
To protect professional status, he demands high education requirements; yet, on the crucial question of
working closely with the local community, the social
worker's educational background has proven of little
assistance. The trend seems to be to draw further
away from community interaction, leaving a serious
gap in relations between communities and their health
institutions. Many times, the medical-social worker
does no more than the clerical duties of getting
prescriptions filled, authorizing bills for medical
payments, etc. Because of these characteristics
among social workers, the addition of a social worker
aide holds great promise. In a manner similar to
job redesign for nursing personnel, the social worker

aide is available to perform various clerical activities. However, more importantly, the social worker aide can become an effective means of starting a dialogue between hospital and community.

CORNELL UNIVERSITY MEDICAL SCHOOL: NURSES LEARNING DOCTORS' FUNCTIONS

Often when the critical shortage of doctors and their skills is discussed, references are made to the possibility of redesigning, i.e., re-allocating some of their duties. For example, Duke University has implemented a two-year program for ex-Army medical corpsmen to train them as "physician assistants." To serve a similar purpose, that of providing a "supporting structure for top-level physicians," Dr. Thomas Killip, Chief of Cardiology at New York Hospital and Professor of Medicine at Cornell University Medical School, has initiated a nurse's training program. The program provides the nurse with a sufficient background to "read electro-cardiograms of patients in acute coronary distress and perform other complex lifesaving tasks formerly done only by physicians."[29]

A significant development in this training program is the joint position statement of the Medical Society of the State of New York, the Hospital Association of the State of New York, and the New State Nurses Association. In part, the statement reads: "It is agreed that in an emergency, and in the absence of and until a physician can take over, a registered professional nurse . . . may initiate the procedure of closed chest cardiac resuscitation (and) that the procedure is primarily a medical procedure." These last few words are an important breakthrough in the medical profession. The "medical procedure" is basically a doctor's prerogative. However, recognizing that doctors cannot be available at all times in hospital wards, that a need for additional patient attention outweighs traditional job structures, these groups have redesigned the responsibilities of both doctor and nurse. There is no reason to now expect a wide-scale attempt to restructure the doctor's function. However, an important point is that these organizations are accepting the practical fact that some activities need not be done only by the doctor; thus, additional personnel find themselves being brought into the growing gap between medical resources and health demands.

SUMMARY

The examples present a broad cross-sectional view of the types of restructuring occurring in the medical and health field (in particular, a number of cases demonstrating the downgrading of job activities to lesser-skilled employees). Where prerogatives had previously been held inviolate, they have been increasingly broken. Similarly, there has been no discernible drop in the quality of care provided where functions have been realigned. In fact, the contrary has occurred. The restructuring of medical activities has improved professional care in almost every instance. One reason for this has been the slowness and caution with which redesign has taken place. Thus, it has become increasingly apparent that restructuring of jobs in the health field is generally feasible.

On the second point, that of developing "new careers," very little has been done by the various health services. There are several obvious reasons for this. First, it has always been difficult for professional groups to accept members who have not followed the accepted steps for entrance. There are numerous legal difficulties that automatically set up barriers for restructuring. These include both city and state licensing procedures for registered nurses, doctors, practical nurses, X-ray technicians, anaesthesiologists, etc., ad infinitum. In some cases, there may exist unions or professional associations that actively oppose development of new career ladders. Specifically relevant to New York City, the civil service has existed and continues to exist as a barrier against new career avenues. Initiated earlier in the century as a means to end discrimination against applicants, it has now become

overly rigid and prohibits most attempts at modern-
ization. Thus, the "new careers" approach faces a
large number of very explicit barriers.

However, as one considers the circumstances,
the new careers chance for implementation does not
appear so doubtful. First, there exists a real
shortage of medical personnel in New York City, and
it is increasing. As explained, a number of restructuring experiments have been attempted and have
worked out quite successfully. In addition, a new
training program at Lincoln Hospital is in the process of developing new job ladders. Although no new
career ladders have been implemented, work is taking
place on several potential programs. This work has
attracted a great deal of interest from other hospital administrative personnel. For these reasons,
the "new careers" approach to better quality care,
reduced hospital personnel shortages, and increased
employment opportunities for the low-income group
holds a great deal of promise for the near future.

NOTES

1. Edith F. Lynton, "The Nonprofessional
Scene," American Child, Vol. 49, No. 1 (Winter,
1967), p. 11.

2. By Arthur Pearl and Frank Riessman (New
York: The Free Press, 1965).

3. Ibid., p. 250.

4. Scientific Resources, Inc., SRI Approach
to Training the Non-professional, presented at Conference on Training the Non-professional, Washington,
D.C., March 15-16, 1967.

5. "The New Non-professional," American Child,
Vol. 49, No. 1 (Winter, 1967), p. 1.

6. Frank Riessman, "The New Careers Concept,"
American Child, Vol. 49, No. 1 (Winter, 1967), p. 4.

7. Pearl and Riessman, op. cit., p. 2.

8. "Forum: Credentials, Careers and Conflicts," American Child, Vol. 49, No. 1 (Winter, 1967), p. 22.

9. Pearl and Riessman, op. cit., p. 4.

10. Ibid., p. 6.

11. Letter to The New York Times, April 27, 1966.

12. William L. Kissick, "Effective Utilization: The Critical Factor in Health Manpower," paper presented at the Ninety-Fourth Annual Meeting of the American Public Health Association, November 2, 1966.

13. See Department of Medicine and Surgery, Veteran's Administration, A Guide for Studying the Utilization of Nursing Service Personnel in Veterans Administration Hospitals (Washington, D.C., March 30, 1961), pp. 1-2.

14. VA Hospital, Dearborn, Michigan, Utilization of Nursing Service Personnel, 1964, p. 1.

15. VA Hospital, Grand Junction, Colorado, A Study of the Utilization of Nursing Service Personnel, 1961, Table 3-A.

16. Ibid., 1962, pp. 2-3.

17. VA Hospital, Dearborn, Michigan, op. cit., p. 17.

18. Ibid., p. 49.

19. Ibid., pp. 51-52.

20. Ibid., p. 2.

21. Lester J. Rosner, Better Utilization of School Health Personnel, Annual Meeting, American Public Health Association, San Francisco, 1966, p. 4.

22. Ibid., p. 13.

23.   Grace McFadden, A Report on an Experiment of Team Nursing in a School Health Survey, Annual Meeting, American Public Health Association, San Francisco, 1966, p. 5.

24.   Louis Hellman, "Let's Use Midwives to Save Babies," Saturday Evening Post, November 21, 1964.

25.   Ibid.

26.   Lydia T. Hall, "Can Nursing Care Hasten Recovery?" The American Journal of Nursing, Vol. 64, No. 6 (June, 1964), reprint.

27.   Ibid.

28.   Tom Levin, Tanya Russell, and Richard Linser, Proposal for an Albert Einstein College of Medicine-Lincoln Hospital Health Careers Program, draft, January 12, 1967, p. 5.

29.   "Nurses Here are Learning Doctors' Work," The New York Times, February 8, 1967.

CHAPTER **3** TOWARD A REDESIGN OF THE
MUNICIPAL HOSPITAL
OCCUPATIONAL STRUCTURE

As with health institutions generally, the
occupational structure of New York City's municipal
hospital system is characterized by extremely limited
mobility between occupations, both vertical and hor-
izontal. Promotional opportunities are limited to
specified occupational groups and usually consist of
less than three steps.* In many cases, there is only
one step and in several others none at all.

For example, in the nursing service group,
there is no direct line of promotion from the lowest-
ranking position, Nurse's Aide, in salary grade 8,
to any other position--not even Practical Nurse in
the next salary grade. The Practical Nurse is in
the same situation; no promotional opportunity exists
for persons in this occupation. Between this category and the next, Staff Nurse, the lowest professional position, there is a wide gulf, the latter being
in grade 16.** From Staff Nurse, one can advance
upward to supervisory positions. However, there is

-----

*"Direct Lines of Promotion" are included in
City job specifications and indicate the combinations
of additional experience and education that will
qualify an incumbent for the next position in that
occupational grouping.

**Currently, the minimum salary for grade 8 is
$4,000 per annum and for grade 16, $6,400. Grade
differentials range from $250 to $300 in that salary
range.

no real distinction in level of technical skill between Staff Nurse and the higher supervisory grades.
There is one exception to the rigidity of the nursing service occupational structure. A Nurse-Midwife
position has been created at salary grade 20, a grade
above Head Nurse and just below Supervisor of Nurses.
This is a specialized position involving the provision
of antepartum, intrapartum, postpartum, and neonatal
care. However, there is no direct line of promotion
to this position; it requires the possession of a
permit to practice issued by the New York City Commissioner of Health.

The absence of intermediate positions between
Nurse's Aide and Practical Nurse on one end of the
scale and Staff Nurse on the other may be prima facie
evidence of poor manpower utilization, particularly
in light of the fact that a number of studies have
shown that staff nurses often perform tasks below
their level of training.*

An examination of the relationships between
positions in other occupational groups also supplies
evidence of insufficient promotional opportunities
and inefficient manpower utilization. For example,
a college or professional nursing diploma is often
required as a prerequisite for the basic position in
a number of groups. These groups, with range of
salary grades and number of direct promotional steps,
are shown in Table 9.

Some of these professionals are assisted by nonprofessional aides, but there is no normal promotional channel between them and no formal training scheme
to encourage mobility. This is the case with respect
to the dental category, where there is a Dental Assistant position at grade 9 and a Dental Hygienist
at grade 13. In addition, there is no direct line of
promotion between these two nonprofessional positions.
Similarly, there is a Library Aide position at Grade

---

*See Chapter 2, especially the Veteran's
Administration studies.

Table 9

DEPARTMENT OF HOSPITALS OCCUPATIONAL GROUPS
REQUIRING COLLEGE DEGREE FOR BASIC POSITION

Occupational Group	Salary Grades	Number of Direct Promotional Steps
Dietician	15-30	6
Pharmacy	17-28	4
Psychologist	19-25	2
Public Health and Safety*	17-21	2
Occupational Therapy	16-19	1
Rehabilitation Counselor	18-20	1
Speech and Hearing Therapy	16	0
Social Worker	17-25	3
Caseworker	14-16	1
Dental	25-30	1
Librarian	15-16	1
Bacteriology	15-25	3
Chemistry	17-27	3
Physics	14-28	4

*Professional nursing degree or Baccalaureate. All others require minimum of Baccalaureate.

Source: Unpublished data from the files of the New York City Departments of Personnel and Hospitals.

7 with no ladder up to the first professional position at grade 15. There is a Laboratory Aide position
at grade 10, but no promotional outlet exists for a
person holding this position. Finally, the position
of Social Work Aide bears a different relationship to
the professional categories than other "aide" positions. This position is for summer employment only
and requires current enrollment in a college or university with a minimum of two years of full-time
work. Obviously, this position exists to encourage
its holders to take full-time jobs in the Department
upon graduation. Because it requires current college
attendance, it cannot be taken as a career-ladder
model.

Although a number of other technical positions
do not require college degrees, job ladders appear
to be inadequately developed for several reasons in
addition to their failure to connect to the professional occupations. On the other end of the spec-
trum, they do not connect with unskilled job categories either, and the number of steps appears too
small internally. Further, virtually all of them
require a high school diploma as a minimum. In some
cases, a diploma from a technical school and a state
license are further requirements. Table 10 shows
these jobs, their salary grades, and direct promotional steps.

DEVELOPING NEW CAREER LADDERS

An illustration of how manpower utilization
could be improved by creating more connections between these occupations was provided in an internal
report of the Department of Hospitals completed several years ago. Regarding laboratory occupations,
the following comment was made:

> In our laboratory services, we currently
> have a laboratory aide, grade 10, and a
> junior scientist in grade 15 as the ba-
> sic positions. Analysis of the typical
> tasks of both of these titles indicates
> that certain duties could be factored out

Table 10

DEPARTMENT OF HOSPITALS NONDEGREE TECHNICAL
OCCUPATIONAL GROUPS

Occupational Group	Salary Grades	Number of Promotional Steps
Physical Therapy	16-19	1
X-ray Technician	11-16	2
Medical Record Librarian	11-15	2
Radiation Technician	11-13	1
Electroencephalograph Technician	11	0
Electrocardiograph Technician	10	0

Source: Unpublished data from the files of the New York City Departments of Personnel and Hospitals.

63

> to provide at least two other titles
> that would provide a more meaningful
> career ladder (when coupled with ap-
> propriate education and experience)
> and would provide better use of per-
> sonnel at their optimum skill level in
> each category. For example, the un-
> skilled duties in the laboratory aide
> title could be assigned to a laboratory
> helper, grade 7; thus, a laboratory
> helper could serve as a promotional op-
> portunity for our various non-skill aide
> titles. It would then allow the labor-
> atory aide to work more effectively on
> the more complicated procedures per-
> formed by those in that title. . . .
> Similarly, it should be possible to con-
> struct a laboratory technician at ap-
> proximately grade 13 who would perform
> the less complicated tasks now included
> at the junior scientist grade 15 level.
> This would provide a promotion oppor-
> tunity for our present laboratory aide
> grade 10 title and would, at the same
> time, free the junior scientist to spend
> more time on the more complex duties.

The report goes on to urge the establishment of
senior levels of aides in dietetic, housekeeping,
and institutional aide titles, along with "appropriate supervisory titles," in order to improve manpower utilization and create new promotional opportunities.

Only detailed job analysis could tell us
whether the same kinds of changes could be made in
other occupational groupings, but the general discontinuity of the structure provides evidence that
is worthy of more detailed investigation. For example, a number of professional jobs such as social
worker, pharmacist, occupational and speech and
hearing therapist, rehabilitation counselor, and
others provide only one or two nonsupervisory grades.
These may well be instances of poor manpower utilization, the presumption being that there are tasks

being performed by persons in these categories that could be performed by nonprofessionals.

That the same kinds of improvement can be made in nonmedical hospital jobs was pointed out in a 1963 study of the Housekeeping Department of three municipal hospitals.[1] Finding that the six existing housekeeping titles "were inadequate to ensure effective organization, proper assignment of responsibility, and adequate supervision," the report advised the creation of two additional positions at the hospital level and two more at the central office. The resulting seven titles at the hospital level would, the authors of the report believed, provide "a range of progressively more responsible positions to accommodate the wide variations in scope of responsibility found within hospital centers and hospitals of the Department." They would also provide considerably more promotional opportunity, including movement to supervisory levels. Finally, the report recommended increased on-the-job training, both for purposes of improving performance and facilitating promotion.

The severe shortages of technical and professional personnel detailed in Chapter 1, the successful experiments in job redesign described in Chapter 2, and the inadequate job ladders discussed above all lead to the reasonable proposition that a systematic occupational analysis of all municipal hospital jobs combined with a large-scale restructuring and training effort would be likely to pay dividends by (1) alleviating manpower shortages and thereby better enabling hospitals to provide "optimal patient care," (2) improving utilization of manpower and thereby lowering the cost per unit of "output," and (3) providing new jobs for the unskilled poor along with considerable opportunity for upward mobility. It is to the task of describing the methodology of such a study that the remainder of this chapter will be devoted.

The principal assumption of this approach is that it is possible to construct an occupational structure from the beginning, unencumbered by

existing practice. The benchmark that will be used
to construct a new occupational structure will be
the view of health manpower as an interrelated whole
rather than as a collection of rigidly separated
categories of personnel. This interrelated whole is
viewed an an input into a system that produces a
particular service or output.

Conceivably the sum of individual tasks could
be "job-packaged" in a number of ways. Each resulting occupational structure could produce the desired
level and quality of output equally as well as any
other. The choice between them would be made on the
basis of goals to be achieved and of exogenous economic forces.

The principal goal is the creation of the maximum number of career ladders for the unskilled poor.
The economic constraints are: (1) production of a
given level of output at least cost, and (2) the
availability of personnel with particular types of
skills. It can be seen that the creation of the
maximum number of career opportunities is in perfect
harmony with the second economic constraint; the
skills in short supply are those that require a considerable amount of training. However, the necessity
to produce output at least cost may be in conflict
with the desire to create a large number of relatively low- or medium-skill jobs. Although it is
logical that the substitution of lower- for higher-
skill jobs will reduce per unit cost of output, it
is conceivable that as the technological limit to
this substitution is reached, the increasing cost of
more and more supervision may offset the savings
resulting from such substitution.

CODIFICATION OF HOSPITAL TASKS

Obviously, then, a large number of factors
must be taken into consideration in the construction
of an "optimal" occupational structure. A coding
system must be devised to reflect all of these factors and applied to each task performed in a hospital. Because of the complexity of the task, it would

be feasible and perhaps necessary once the coding
stage is completed to subject the results to automat-
ic data processing. Once methodology and programing
procedures are worked out, the computer could then
be instructed to produce one or more occupational
structures that most closely fit the ends being
sought.

Job Analysis

The first step in the study would be a traditional job analysis of all hospital occupations. The
result of this analysis could be the identification
of the tasks that comprise each job, an estimate of
the length of time spent by each employee on each
thing he does and where he does it, and identification of the skills, knowledge, ability, and responsibility required for successful performance of each
task. There are basically two methods that can be
used in carrying out a job analysis. One of them,
practiced by the U.S. Bureau of Employment Security,
uses trained job analysts who analyze the job through
direct observation and by interviewing the employee
in question, his supervisor, or other persons who
have knowledge of the job.

The other, as developed by Veteran's Administration hospitals, is called the "work-diary" technique. Under this method, the personnel whose activities are being studied are required to record
them, usually at five-minute intervals. Both methods,
of course, can be supplemented by supervisory analysis and use of job descriptions, training manuals,
and related material.

The major advantage of the work-diary method
is that it can be done at relatively low cost since
no additional persons need be employed for that
purpose. On the other hand, its principal limitation arises from the fact that the employee whose
activities are being studied must spend time in recording them. To overcome this, the recording must
be as simple as possible and require a minimum
amount of time. Further, this method has been used
mainly to study professional nursing activities. It

presumes a reasonable educational level and might,
therefore, not be appropriate for low-level jobs.
It is also obvious that the method is only suitable
in cases where activity is intermittent. Some persons engaging in operating or emergency room activities would, of course, not be able to find even
the minimal amount of time necessary to record their
activities.

The use of a job analyst would provide a solution to some of these difficulties. The major disadvantage of this method, however, is that it is
rather costly. The Bureau of Employment Security,
which is currently doing a job analysis study in
some 35 hospitals throughout the country, has estimated that the job analysis itself requires one man-
day per job for observation plus another man-day for
transcribing the results on standard forms. Perhaps
an optimum approach in a hospital job analysis would
be to use the work-diary method for most professional
nursing jobs, where the methodology has been widely
practiced and refined, and to use trained job analysts
for all other occupations. Since professional nursing employees represent about 10 per cent of all employees, including nonmedical personnel, this will
reduce the over-all cost of the program by a significant amount. The work-diary method might also be
extended to other professional personnel as well; how
widely it is applicable can best be determined by
experimentation.

Coding of the tasks that go to make up each
occupation can follow the Veteran's Administration
model for nursing service personnel, which uses 8
one-digit classifications. These are: Waiting Time,
Direct Nursing Care, Indirect Nursing Care, Security
for All, Coordinating Professional Services, Coordinating Hospital Technical Services, Coordinating Institutional Services, Personnel Services. Further
breakdowns are made on a two- and three-digit basis.
For our purposes, two may be adequate, although it
is conceivable that three may be required.*

---

*For the Veteran's Administration two-digit
breakdown, see Appendix.

Following this "first-level" classification,
each task or duty must be coded further on the basis
of other criteria that will essentially determine
the degree to which the entire occupational structure
can be redesigned. At this stage, because of time
and technical limitations, it is not possible to develop a sophisticated and comprehensive coding scheme.
What can be done, however, is to list in some detail
the factors that should be included and how they can
best be measured.

Perhaps the most important factor is a measure
of the content of each task in terms of what it demands of the worker in knowledge and need for independent action. Each of these two characteristics
could be broken down into at least five, possibly
six or more, gradations. With respect to knowledge,
for example, these might be based on, in the absence
of more concrete data, estimates of training requirements. The highest level of knowledge required would
be that conferred by a doctorate, either M.D. or
Ph.D. The next would be represented by a bachelor's
or master's degree. Next, a two-year associate degree, then vocational or technical training, then
on-the-job training, the latter perhaps graded by
length of time. Each gradation would presume liter-
acy but would not necessarily require evidence of
elementary or high school graduation.[2] Alternatively,
it might be possible to develop codes based on actual
content, such as chemistry or English, and the level
of content needed. The characteristic "need for independent action" encompasses supervisory responsibilities and, especially in the case of nurses, responsibility for coordinating all the various professional services. It could be evaluated in much the
same way as knowledge, with level of education or
training serving as a proxy for the grades "high,"
"medium," "low," and "none." What should be stressed
here is that current educational requirements are
being used only as scales for measurement in the construction of a new occupational structure. In terms
of creation of career ladders under a redesigned system of jobs, traditional educational requirements
need not be binding. Experience and on-the-job training equivalents need to be developed as alternatives

to formal degree and diploma programs in order to
facilitate upward movement.

Efficiency of operation demands that there be
similarity of technological content among the tasks
that make up a job, that they be sequentially related,
and that there be an optimal amount of task repeti-
tion. Therefore, tasks and duties should be grouped
so that the employee assigned to the work can use his
highest skills and abilities to the maximum extent
and so that there is an even and economical flow of
work. Tasks and duties should thus be as near the
same skill level as possible, similar in function
and during the same part of the 24-hour period. We
must, therefore, code each task on the basis of
homogeneity with other tasks in a functional sense.
This is differentiated from the coding of skill and
knowledge. It is more an industrial engineering
problem of work simplification and physical flow than
of ability to satisfactorily perform the task.

Another factor to be considered is whether a
particular task can be characterized as being conven-
ventionally performed by males or by females, even
though it might be able to be done by either. It is
more difficult to classify tasks in this way than
jobs, but conceivably it can be done. The breakdown
should be on a three-way basis--that is, male, female,
or either. This coding should also take into account
the fact that some tasks can only be performed by
males in that they require a particular level of
strength.

Although there has been some desirable erosion
in the distinction between jobs by sex, one would be
unrealistic to ignore this factor in an over-all view
of the municipal hospital occupational structure.
What might be learned in the process, however, is
what it is that constitutes a male or female job. If
we learn, for example, that any job that has, say,
more than 60 per cent of its tasks classified as female is usually considered a "female job," then we
have information vital for the restructuring process.
We might want to instruct the computer to "desex"
jobs--that is, give no job more than 59 per cent male

or female tasks. We may, on the other hand, choose
to withhold any instructions about sex from the computer. If so, we can view the results to see whether
they are overbalanced in favor of one sex or another
and whether this overbalance is unrealistic in view
of labor supply conditions.

We must also associate cost estimates with each
task. These will be closely associated with job content and might be coded on a descending scale such as
6 for M.D. and Ph.D., 5 for baccalaureate, etc. If
possible, the gradations should be even finer with
two or three cost grades for each level of job content.

Staff Nurse/Patient Relationship

Another important factor that must be considered in the coding of job tasks is the traditional
staff nurse/patient relationship. It has been pointed out that, even though the bedside nurse may be
performing some duties that do not ostensibly require
her level of education and training, the rapport that
is created by continual contact may form the basis
for the application of the nurse's clinical and di-
agnostic skills. Even the most humble task could be
considered part of a continuum of tasks, all of which
are dependent on all others in a psychological sense.
The advocates of this point of view deplore the transfer of direct patient care to ancillary personnel,
resulting only in intermittent contact of patients
and professional nurse. The system, says Frances
Reiter, "has resulted in a relative--and sometimes
absolute--lack of professional nursing care for patients."[3] Lydia E. Hall states, "With this increasing trend, patients receive from professional nursing
second class doctoring; and from practical nurses,
second class nursing."[4] Both Dean Reiter and Mrs.
Hall argue that the nucleus of nursing practice is
"nurturing" or "the mother role." Thus, personal services such as bathing, toileting, dressing, positioning, etc., are fundamental and necessary because the
"whole patient" must be treated, not merely his illness. Nurturing is of course only a part of the job.
The close relationship that results from it facilitates

the application of the other aspects of the professional's job--medical care and counseling. All are
considered part of an inseparable whole; no one can
be broken off without affecting the quality of another.

        This approach to nursing has, as mentioned in
Chapter 2, been applied by Mrs. Hall at the Loeb Center for Nursing and Rehabilitation, the extended care
unit of Montefiore Hospital. Here, virtually all
patient care is provided by professional nurses; the
only auxiliary personnel are a ward secretary and
some messenger-attendants. Other staff includes medical consultants, therapists, social workers, and
dieticians, all of whose services are coordinated
by the nurse. Patients at Loeb are "out of biological crises, but have not reached a stage when they
may leave the institutional setting where professional
care for most specialties is available on call. Here
they can derive the greatest benefit from professional
nursing care and teaching in their efforts to achieve
recovery and restoration."[5]

        Obviously--unless, as previously suggested, the
Loeb nurse is considered to be a new or "additive
position"*--this concept and the "new careers" idea
are somewhat exclusive of each other, at least with
reference to patient care. "New careers" assumes a
hierarchy of tasks within the total job, some of which
can be adequately performed by nonprofessionals. The
nurse-clinician concept argues that all patient care
must be treated as a whole.

        The two approaches can perhaps be reconciled by
examining particular tasks in greater detail to see
if there is a relationship between personal care and
medical care in each case. For example, while dispensing of medication may be closely related to cure
in that the nurse has an opportunity to discuss the
need for the medication, its side effects, and results, it is more difficult to make such a case for

_____

        *See Chapter 2.

fetching water, emptying bedpans, positioning the patient, and the like. There is no indication that a strong case has been made for each activity; rather, it is assumed that all contact with the patient must be made by the professional nurse. Even the analogy of "mother-substitute" provided by Dean Reiter does not permit that conclusion. Children, after all, do come into contact with teachers, tradesmen, domestics, and relatives. This extended interaction must certainly be as necessary to his emotional stability as the existence of a comforting mother.

The issue, in our view, remains open. After each task is examined, a decision can be made to what degree it must be allied with tasks that require formal education or training. Coding would then be identical with the coding of the linked task. That is, if dispensing of medication is considered to be linked to a task such as "observing signs, symptoms, reactions," it should be coded at a bachelor's or associate degree level.

This problem is associated with a classic debate in the field of industrial job design. The problem concerns itself with the trade-offs between benefits from specialization and division of labor on one hand and benefits from increased worker satisfaction due to job enlargement--that is, enlarging their scope to capture the interest of workers. The enlargement can be accomplished by adding related or sequential activities or by adding extra dimensions such as supervision and participation in decision-making. The advocates of job enlargement assert that work simplification has sometimes been carried to the point where jobs become repetitious and dull. The worker feels unimportant, he receives little or no satisfaction from his job, his morale sags, and productivity is adversely affected. Although the situation can sometimes be alleviated by human relations and welfare activities, the work enlargers feel that it is possible to design jobs that are both mechanically efficient and efficient from the standpoint of the psychological needs of the individual performing the work.

The Loeb Center approach may be considered job
enlargement for professional nurses (if not for the
messenger-attendants), but the relationship of the
"new careers" concept to job enlargement is actually
more complex. Under "new careers," increased specialization will take place in some of the more
skilled occupations, but the degree of specialization
will in most cases remain unchanged for the unskilled
jobs that tend to be quite specialized now. What will
happen in the latter case is that more demanding
tasks, usually less routine in nature, will be sub-
stituted for simpler ones, usually more routine. We
may view this as a process of job enlargement from
the horizon of the worker; certainly it cannot be
seen as a case of extreme specialization of labor
such as is sometimes seen in industrial plants, nor
is it likely to lead to less job satisfaction.

And that is the important question. If we now
go beyond the job design itself and look at the "new
careers" idea in its entire context, we can hopefully
predict not only greater technological efficiency,
but greater job satisfaction and, therefore, greater
human efficiency as well. For a career job, closely
related to others in the work sequence, can be assumed to be a more meaningful unit of activity for
the worker if it allows him to better perceive the
value of his contribution to the hospital, to the
community, and to society. It can be assumed to be
more meaningful if it is perceived as containing some
degree of prestige within the hospital and community,
if it requires maximum utilization of the worker's
skills and abilities, if it provides measures of performance to the individual, and if it provides significant incentives and promotional opportunities.
All of these "new careers" can provide. And if we can
take the results of one study as representative of
low-skilled employees, these things are badly needed.
Nurse's aides at St. Vincent's Hospital in New York
City were found to have had strong dissatisfactions
with their jobs because of frustration in striving
for recognition and acceptance. They were interested
in receiving further training, in career opportunities, in understanding the nature of the patients'
illnesses, in working more directly with patients--

in general, in being part of a nursing team rather than maids or porters. They considered that their most important duties were "routing nursing services and comfort and hygiene of patients."[6] A program that emphasizes that aspect of their jobs cannot but improve morale and efficiency.

This might not be the case with staff nurses who would, under a job redesign, be most likely performing more specialized, albeit less routine duties. Some difficulties might be created, particularly when these more specialized duties consist of managing, coordinating, and supervising care provided by nonprofessionals. For there is some evidence that a number of staff nurses neither desire nor feel equipped to supervise auxiliary personnel. Rather, they prefer to provide direct patient care and, when engaged in administrative and supervisory work, feel they are not practicing nursing as they envisioned it nor as it was taught in the classroom.[7] On the other hand, to the degree that staff nurses are relieved of the more routine bedside duties and are allowed to devote more time to the particular patient care skills for which they alone are qualified, one can reasonably expect an improvement in morale and a more positive attitude toward the job. Certainly this has often occurred as nurses have been relieved of routine clerical tasks as a result of the creation of the ward manager position.

Perhaps the answer to the complex relationship between the staff nurse and auxiliary personnel lies in the restructuring of nursing education and in further specialization on the professional level. Graduates of four- or five-year baccalaureate programs or their "new careers" equivalent could receive training in teaching, administration, and supervision as part of these programs. They would exercise these functions in connection with two- or three-year program professionals specializing in patient care with nonprofessionals performing the more routine duties connected with it. The point here is that administration and supervision would become normal tasks on the higher levels of the nursing ladder. Those who had no taste for it could limit themselves to

clinical positions and to the smaller amount of training connected with them.

Basic Classification Codes

To summarize, the basic codes to be used in the
classification of job tasks are as follows:

A. Activity classification code. Two-digit
    breakdown following Veteran's Administra-
    tion model for nursing personnel, but
    extended to encompass other types of jobs.
    Includes estimate of time spent on each
    task and physical location of task.

B. Knowledge required for successful perform-
    ance by academic equivalent:

    1. M.D. or Ph.D.
    2. Bachelor's or Master's degree
    3. Two-year associate degree
    4. Vocational or technical training
    5. On-the-job training or by actual con-
            tent and level

C. Need for independent action:

    1. Supervisory or administrative
    2. High
    3. Medium
    4. Low
    5. None

D. Homogeneity of tasks in functional sense:

    1. Inseparable
    2. Allied
    3. Not allied
    4. Incompatible

            or

    1. Similar technological content
    2. Allied
    3. Dissimilar

and

1. Sequentially related
2. Not sequentially related

E. Time of day performed:

1. Day shift
2. Night shift

F. Male or female activity:

1. Male
2. Female
3. Either

G. Cost estimates: code inversely to knowledge code, with possible finer breakdown.

H. Alliance with tasks requiring higher
levels of knowledge: code as most difficult task.

This listing is not meant to be comprehensive; rather,
it is a preliminary guide for thinking about the
problem. Undoubtedly, persons more familiar with
hospital activities can improve it and make it a
more sophisticated device for a detailed analysis of
the occupational structure. This particular coding
model is designed to facilitate the production of an
occupational structure emphasizing the maximum number
of nonprofessional career ladders. With additions,
it can be made to serve other purposes. For example,
it might be a matter of public policy to redesign
jobs for older workers or handicapped workers. In
such cases, additional codes could be added to rate
tasks on the basis of motor abilities, numerical and
spatial aptitudes, and visual perception required.
Tasks could then be combined by computer to produce
jobs whose physical content could be handled by these
particular workers.[8]

IMPLICATIONS OF JOB REDESIGN

A new kind of hospital occupational structure will, of course, have important implications for education and training for health occupations. There will be a need to carefully analyze the skills and knowledge needed by each category of worker and evolve from it a comprehensive educational and training program coordinated with the occupational structure itself. Among other things, it will consist of both formal and clinical training, and it will be organized so that it will facilitate movement along and between job ladders. The upward movement will be very gradual, more of a movement on an inclined plane than on a ladder. The training should be designed to allow trainees to take a small number of steps, rather than a large jump. It will undoubtedly involve cooperative arrangements between hospitals and community educational institutions and will be built into the job content rather than stand outside of it. This means that each employee, or perhaps each employee desiring promotion, will be obliged to be enrolled in a program designed to improve his skill and to aid his advancement. The training should be costless to the employee and, if possible, take place during his working hours. The emergence of the publicly supported community college with emphasis on vocational and professional training is of considerable significance for such an educational program. These institutions, under public support, are by philosophy and location well suited to undertake the formal educational portion of the program whereas the hospitals can handle the clinical portion. Among the advantages of such a division is the opportunity to relieve the hospitals of some of their educational costs. It seems appropriate to charge basic educational costs to the general community rather than to the users of hospital beds, particularly in a community like New York City which provides an enormous amount of vocational education through higher education and other expenditures.

Because New York City's community colleges have already begun planning for an extensive program of health careers training, adapting such a program to

provide the educational support for a redesigned occupational structure with a "new careers" orientation
should not be difficult. Among the major functions
of the proposed Health Careers Center for City University are both "developing and operating programs
of instruction leading to appropriate degrees in
health fields not now offered at any City University
college" and "stimulating the operation of special
programs to encourage the disadvantaged to enter
health careers, and to provide counseling and remedi-
al work necessary for entry level jobs, retraining
and upward mobility."[9]

The University of the State of New York has
also been concerned with the development of health
careers educational programs in its community colleges. In its planning, it has attempted to "identify appropriate curriculum patterns for health career programs," "prepare community college teachers
to carry out the programs thus identified," and "establish pilot programs in selected community colleges
for purposes of testing the new curriculums and eval-
uating the graduates by means of on-the-job follow-up
studies."[10] Here, too, there is a developing program
that can be drawn upon to develop appropriate educational programs for a redesigned occupational structure. A third training project that would seem also
to have great potential as a support for redesign is
the proposed Albert Einstein College of Medicine
Health Careers Institute. It, in fact, is closely
related to the "new careers" concept since it has
drawn both on the idea and on the applications of it
at Lincoln Hospital.

Naturally, job redesign can be expected to have
some effect on the traditional training programs for
physicians, registered nurses, pharmacists, and others,
but the effect should only be minimal. The jobs at
the top of the occupational ladder will still require
technical mastery--the existing training is geared to
providing this. The greatest effect of job redesign
on these persons will be on the job. It will relieve
them of some tasks they may have been doing as by-
products of their training but which could be done
as well by a person trained in a different way. The

new occupational structure might have a different
kind of effect, however, on the activities of professionals. Because on-the-job training will be a more
organic part of hospital operation at all levels,
they will, along with virtually everyone else, have
new responsibilities as trainers in addition to being
trainees. There will also be increased supervisory
responsibility all along the line, supervision in
some ways being indistinguishable from the training
function. Even now, it has been asserted that there
are not enough qualified supervisors; with systematic
job redesign, it becomes even more important to remedy this situation.

It must also be recognized that any program
that proposes significant innovations must have the
cooperation of professional accrediting organizations,
trade unions, and governmental agencies, particularly
those concerned with licensing, revising standards,
and changing job content.

Of these groups in New York City, trade unions
will probably cooperate most readily. District Council 37 of the American Federation of State, County,
and Municipal Employees Union is the bargaining representative for housekeeping, catering, and other nonprofessional employees in the municipal hospitals,
including nurse's aides. The union has taken an active part in designing and sponsoring upgrading programs, including one designed to advance nurse's aides
to licensed practical nurses, operating and delivery
room technicians, oxygen therapy technicians, and
ambulance attendants. Because most unionized employees
are at the bottom of the occupational ladder, they and
their union can be assumed to have no vested interest
in the existing job structure. There is, thus, every
reason to believe that the development of new subprofessional positions, job ladders, and training programs will elicit their enthusiastic cooperation.

The case is not so clear for other occupational
groups. Licensing and accreditation have as often
been used as pure economic devices to restrict supply
and increase rewards as they have been used as methods
to protect the public. Were demand for health services

not increasing as rapidly as it is, one might despair of changing these requirements.[11] But with an unprecedented demand for all health service skills, professional organizations and licensing agencies can probably be induced to make a realistic appraisal of existing requirements with a view toward finding alternative ways of satisfying them through combinations of experience, training, and education. An example of this type of cooperation was provided by the American Occupational Therapy Association and the State University Health Careers Project jointly attempting to establish "curriculum guidelines and objectives" for a community college program in occupational therapy assisting.[12]

Nevertheless, one should not be overly sanguine about the possibilities of wholehearted cooperation. The real difficulties in accomplishing this should be frankly recognized. Although the Health Careers Project had success with the Occupational Therapy Association, its Advisory Committee recommended that the project refrain from the development of a program for a new dental auxiliary occupation since it might cause "strained professional relationships."[13] The drive by the American Nurses' Association for universal baccalaureate level nurse's training is another example of a possible conflict between professional association demands and the development of subprofessional categories. These problems must be dealt with as they arise and on an individual basis. Although not all resistance will be based on fear of layoffs resulting from redesigning jobs, some will undoubtedly be based on that belief. Greater cooperation may, therefore, be ensured by a guarantee that no layoff and no reduction in pay grade will result from the introduction of the program.

Finally, any civil service requirements that present significant barriers to a new careers program should be overcome. These include unrealistic entrance qualifications;* the use of written tests

---

*Discussed in greater detail in Chapter 4.

that tend to discriminate against the poor who fre-
quently lack the skills necessary for successful performance on these tests; disqualifying factors such
as arrests, convictions, alcoholism, use of narcotics,
and poor work history; and the lengthy civil service
process itself requiring application, testing, interview, and notification, which sometimes works to dis-
courage applicants. In addition to eliminating these
barriers, it has been proposed that credit be given
for such things as residing in certain neighborhoods
where it is considered an important part of the job--
for example, neighborhood aides and counselor aides--
and that one year's temporary or provisional employment be provided, after which normal civil service
standards would prevail.[14]

Because we have been stressing the more mechan-
ical aspects of job redesign, it is desirable to men-
tion at least once that the total operational picture
must always be kept in mind. Otherwise, sequence of
operations may be upset and work distribution patterns
destroyed. A careful check with all who know the
operations, scheduling, and routing must be made. Also, it may be a good idea to put new jobs into effect
gradually. This will permit adjustment in job design
as needed changes become apparent.

In short, a program of job evaluation, occupational redesign, and curriculum development must be
the joint product of all groups affected by it. The
technical solution is not enough; to work, it requires
the endorsement of educational institutions, trade
unions, professional associations, and government
agencies and, finally, intelligent implementation by
professional health workers. With such endorsement
and implementation, we can hope to make a significant
contribution toward alleviating the chronic skill
shortages in the City's hospitals and by doing so improve the quality and quantity of the services the
hospitals provide.

NOTES

1. Cresap, McCormick, and Paget, Study of Housekeeping Titles, Report to the New York City Department of Hospitals, June 25, 1963.

2. This classification scheme was suggested by Darrel J. Mase in "The Utilization of Mindpower," a paper presented to the American Public Health Association, Health Manpower Section, November 2, 1966.

3. "The Nurse-Clinician," American Journal of Nursing, February, 1966, p. 278.

4. Lydia E. Hall, "Nursing - What is it?" The Canadian Nurse, February, 1964.

5. "Information on the Loeb Center for Nursing and Rehabilitation" (Mimeograph, January 22, 1963).

6. U.S. Department of Health, Education and Welfare, Public Health Service, Hospital Personnel, Report of a Personnel Research Project (Washington, D.C.: U.S. Government Printing Office, 1964), pp. 61-62.

7. Ibid., pp. 58-59, and Genrose Alfano, "Administration Means Working with Nurses," American Journal of Nursing, Vol. 64, No. 6 (June, 1964).

8. See Solomon Barkin, "Job Redesign: A Technique for an Era of Full Employment," in Manpower in the United States, William Haber, et al. (New York: Harper, 1954).

9. "Proposal: That a Health Careers Center be Established in the City University of New York," Draft Three (Mimeograph, March 13, 1967), p. 2.

10. "Technicians for the Health Field: A Community College Health Careers Project," final report on Phase I of the Community College Health Careers Project, University of the State of New York, October 1, 1964-March 31, 1966, p. 1.

11.   See the paper by Richard Brief, <u>Licensing and Employment in New York City</u>, a report of Project Labor Market, GBA/NYU (New York, June, 1968). (Mimeograph.)

12.   "Technicians for the Health Field," <u>op. cit</u>., p. 20.

13.   <u>Ibid</u>., p. 17.

14.   Greenleigh Associates, Inc., "Summary Report: Potential for Demonstration Community Employment Programs in Eight Communities," New York, December 15, 1966.

CHAPTER **4** OTHER CITY AGENCIES AND
THE "NEW CAREERS" CONCEPT

Although vastly overshadowed by the manpower
needs of the Department of Hospitals, many other City
agencies also face shortages of professional and
technical employees. Those with particularly trouble-
some problems are the departments of Parks, Finance,
Buildings, Health, Highways, Public Works, Water Supply, and Welfare, the Housing Authority, and the three
public library systems.

It is difficult to get a complete accounting of
unfilled vacancies and present and future needs for
City departments; there are, however, several studies
that approach the question from slightly different
angles. When viewed together, they provide reasonably good quantitative estimates of shortages and pin-
point the types of jobs where shortages are most acute
and the departments that contain significant numbers
of these jobs.

PROFESSIONAL MANPOWER SHORTAGES IN NEW YORK CITY

The Brookings Institution Study

In the 1963 Brookings Institution study Professional Personnel for the City of New York, it was
reported that vacancies in the professional, technical, and managerial categories were more than 20 per
cent. The problems with respect to attorneys, accountants, civil engineers, and architects were noncompetitive pay scales and unattractive working conditions, but shortages of health service workers,
social workers, and some types of engineers, statis-
ticians, planners, and actuaries were ascribed to an
insufficient supply of the particular skill.[1]

The policy implication of this is that job redesign should not be considered a means of relieving
shortages in certain job categories until salary
rates are brought up to market levels. If the shortages persist, job redesign along the lines indicated
in the previous chapters seems warranted, if it can
be applied.

New York City Department of Personnel Survey

In early 1967, the Department of Personnel conducted a survey of manpower needs designed to determine (1) current shortages, (2) additional staffing
needs through 1971, (3) the effects of new programs,
administrative reorganization, and technological
change on manpower needs, and (4) potentialities for
use of part-time and temporary personnel. Although
the study is yet incomplete in that a number of re-
turns from some of the larger departments are not
yet available, it nevertheless reveals some significant problem areas.

The Department of Health, for example, has many
of the occupational titles used in the Department of
Hospitals and shows shortages in all of them despite
fairly heavy employment of provisional employees.
Table 11 shows, for a number of these occupations,
budgeted and filled positions as of January 1, 1967,
the number of persons who will have to be hired to
December 31, 1971, to fill new positions and replace
employees who leave the agency, expected shortages
during the next five years, and the turnover rate
during calendar 1966.

To interpret this data, several things should
be taken into account. First, the tally is in no way
complete since the departments were asked for data
covering "key titles" only. This is defined as the
titles covering about 85 per cent of "normal staffing
requirements." Second, even though vacancies may
appear, this may be a result not of inability to recruit qualified employees but the result of a "job
freeze"--that is, a Budget Bureau restriction on filling vacancies. There is, thus, no way of telling
from this information alone what is the cause of a

Table 11

PERSONNEL DATA FOR THE DEPARTMENT OF HEALTH

	Positions Budgeted 1/1/67	Positions Filled 1/1/67*	Employees Needed to 12/31/71	Expected Vacancies Next Five Years	1966 Turn-over Rate
Dental Hygienist	174	168	217	n.a.	12%
Head Nurse (Public Health) ⎫ Staff Nurse ⎬	668	551	290	100	26
Junior Bacteriologist	107	85	27	n.a.	14
Public Health Assistant	538	517	100	n.a.	10
Public Health Sanitarian	286	279	9	n.a.	2
Senior Public Health Sanitarian	89	86	0	n.a.	3
Supervisor of Nurses (Public Health)	75	71	8	n.a.	11
Civil Engineer (Sanitary)	n.a.	n.a.	n.a.	3	n.a.
Consultant (Public Health Social Work)	n.a.	n.a.	n.a.	13	n.a.
Physical Therapist	n.a.	n.a.	n.a.	10	n.a.
Nutritionist	n.a.	n.a.	n.a.	8	n.a.

"n.a."--not available.
*Includes provisional employees.

particular vacancy. It is a reasonable assumption,
however, that the vast bulk of them are the result
of hiring problems rather than administrative restrictions.

From a short-range point of view, of most significance is the difference between budgeted and
filled positions, i.e., current vacancies. From a
long-run view, the most useful data appears in the
"Employees Needed to 12/31/71" column. This shows
the number of hirings that will have to take place
to offset normal turnover and to fill newly created
positions. Where the figure is high relative to the
existing budgeted positions, as in the case of Dental
Hygienists and Nurses, it indicates that job redesign
may be a useful method of easing the hiring problems
expected in the next five years.

Data for other departments is more sketchy and
defies generalization, except in the case of a few
positions. Engineering shortages, for example, appear to be significant. Of 197 budgeted positions
in the Planning Commission, the Traffic Department,
and the Borough Presidents' offices, 35 were vacant.
The Traffic Department reported that as a result of
the expansion of new programs it expected to have 35
new engineering positions and 35 new Highway Trans-
portation Specialists. But because of the "shortage
of engineers with traffic engineering education or
experience," the Department expected a shortage of
about 50 employees in these categories.

Although the Department of Sanitation did not
supply current data on engineers, it reported that
with the development of its engineering branch between 50 and 100 new positions in the fields of civil,
sanitary, automotive, marine, and air pollution engineering fields would be created in a one- to two-
year period.

While accountants do not appear to be in such
short supply as engineers, almost all departments
using significant numbers of them report shortages.
The Office of the Comptroller showed 52 vacancies
of 245 budgeted positions with 11 new employees needed

in 1967 because of new positions and turnover. The
Housing Authority showed 7 vacancies out of 127 positions with 12 new employees needed this year. The
Department of Finance had no vacancies in its 299
budgeted accounting positions, but 16 of the incum-
bents were provisional employees. The Department
had, however, 50 new accounting positions to fill in
1967 and 150 others, including 12 methods analysts,
8 programmers, and 8 computer analysts. With respect
to the latter, the Department of Education reported
difficulty in recruiting "adequately trained" computer
programmers and in retaining the services of systems
analysts trained in that agency "due to higher salaries available in private industry." It can be expected that as City agencies make increased use of
these titles, these problems will tend to become more
general.

Another general shortage that becomes apparent
from the Department of Personnel study is in the field
of social work. The Housing Authority has 6 vacancies
of 29 positions and expects to have to hire about 20
new employees in this and future years because of separations. In 1966, the Department had 24 separations
in this category. The Department of Correction had
13 caseworkers to fill 16 positions but needs 20 more
employees this year as the result of turnover and the
creation of new positions. In subsequent years, it
expects separations to average 6 employees per year
and expects a total of 8 new positions to December
31, 1971. The shortage of rehabilitation counselors
in this department is even more acute than that of
caseworkers. Here only 6 of 12 positions are filled
at present and 30 new positions have been provided
in the 1967-68 budget. Separations in future years
are expected to average about 3 per year. The Department of Relocation, which has 9 of 13 social
worker positions filled, has obtained approval to
use caseworkers to relieve this shortage. These
persons will work under the supervision of a social
worker or social work supervisor. The Department
expects that as relocation activities increase, all
of these positions will require significant increases
in numbers. A related position in the Housing and
Redevelopment Board, community organization specialist,

seems the most difficult of all to fill, perhaps because it is a relatively new occupation. Of 6 budgeted positions, none at all was filled on January
1, 1968.

The remaining shortages reported were in categories particular to the departments reporting them.
The Department of Relocation, for one, stated that
it had chronic difficulty in recruiting in the real
estate manager position. Here, 71 of 85 positions
were filled, but only 33 by permanent employees.
The Department has, however, been granted the use of
a Relocation Aide title. This position will be open
to high school graduates; its holder is expected to
perform the simpler duties of the real estate manager,
under his direction. After two years, the aide would
become eligible to take the Civil Service Examination
for real estate manager.

As is well known, the Police Department has a
persistent problem of recruiting patrolmen. At the
moment, there are about 800 vacancies of a total of
24,475 budgeted positions. In addition to filling
these, 1,000 new positions have been provided in the
1967-68 budget and about 1,200 separations are expected this year and in each of the next four years.
It is clear that, in this department, efficiencies
that can be made by using clerical employees and
other civilians to replace patrolmen in routine duties
will have large payoffs, both in reduced cost and
improved police service.

In the Department of Personnel manpower survey,
an attempt was made to determine the extent to which
the City departments could make use of temporary and
part-time personnel. The need for temporary employees
seems to be extremely limited since most of the departments that expressed interest could use only a
few persons, mainly summer replacements in clerical
jobs. A few others, such as Finance and Purchase,
stated that they could use temporary employees during
peak periods, but over-all their needs were not large.
The one department that indicated that widespread use
could be made of temporaries was the Department of
Relocation, which has need of employees totaling 55

man-years.* All of these jobs are in the category
of Relocation Aide; the duties consist of assisting
in packing and moving, handling night emergencies,
and collecting pre- and post-relocation data.

On the other hand, if the answers of the re-
sponding agencies are typical of all of them, there
seems to be considerable opportunity for part-time
employment. The Department of Hospitals, for example,
indicated that they are able to use part-time employees as staff nurses, occupational therapists,
physical therapists, social workers, and dietary institutional and housekeeping aides and have budget
lines for them. They would also like to hire part-
time people as dieticians, housekeepers, pharmacists,
stenographers, and typists, but do not have the budget lines to do so. As a general principle, instead
of modifying full-time positions to part-time, the
Department would like the flexibility to fill all
positions with one full-time person or two part-time
persons.

The Department of Health also expressed interest in part-time personnel, estimating about 250
man-years available in nursing, dental assistant,
and clerical classifications. Other departments indicating significant possible use were Education, 50
man-years in clerical positions; Relocation and Housing Authority, an undetermined number of social workers; and the Housing and Redevelopment Board, 10 man-
years in the Urban Renewal Aide category. Several
other smaller agencies expressed need for part-time
persons in amounts ranging from one to seven man-
years.

On the basis of this data, we can reasonably
conclude that part-time employment by City agencies
could be extensive were these agencies to investigate
and develop such opportunities, including the possibility of breaking full-time positions into two or
more part-time jobs.

---

*One man-year = 1,750 man-hours (250 days x
7 hours).

Part-time work is particularly appropriate for
female heads-of-households who, under new Department
of Welfare regulations, may be able to supplement
aid-to-dependent-children grants and for high school
youths who might supplement family income as they
simultaneously develop their future earning capacity.
All City agencies should be urged to develop such
positions consistent with their needs and the state
of the labor market.

Budgeted vs. Filled Positions, Fiscal 1965

The conclusions reached in the Brookings and
Department of Personnel surveys are supported by our
own study of budgeted and filled positions in selected departments and selected occupations in fiscal
1965. The departments for which data was gathered
were those in which shortages were judged to be most
acute. The jobs were in most cases skilled, technical, and professional or others where redesign might
be a possibility. The numbers of employees were secured from payroll data; these were compared with
the number budgeted in each category. Because it is
not meaningful to list data for the thousands of job
categories, many of which have fewer than five employees in each department, highlights of the data
will be presented, department by department, with
emphasis on categories where there are major shortages.*

---

*It should be pointed out that the data are
not exact because of the problems connected with
deriving employment figures from aggregate payroll
data and the difficulties of reconciling these with
the data presented in the Executive Budget. Another
problem arises from the fact that some jobs are paid
from Capital Budget special funds and therefore do
not appear in the Executive Budget but do appear in
payroll data. Where this is the case, the category
is not discussed since shortages, if they exist,
would be hidden.

In the Department of Health, the expected shortages in technical categories are present. These are recapitulated in Table 12.

In addition to the general skill shortages, it is interesting to note a large number of vacancies among Public Health Assistants, who perform nonprofessional duties and whose average annual salary, at that time, was less than $4,000. We are not able to provide the reason or reasons for this problem, but we can suggest the hypothesis that it is the dead-endedness of this and similar jobs in the municipal hospitals and elsewhere which contributes to shortages in the face of a high unemployment rate among unskilled persons.

The Department of Welfare's serious shortage of social investigators is well known, but the fact that it has a large number of vacancies virtually across the board is not common knowledge. Table 13 shows these vacancies for occupational groups and job classifications where there are a reasonably large number of persons involved.

The shortages of clerical and stenographic employees found in the Department of Welfare are typical of some other departments as well. In the Department of Hospitals, for example, there is a shortage of about 200 clerks and 75 stenographers. These vacancies and those in other departments are shown in Table 14.

Other departments, however, show few or no vacancies in these two classifications. The shortages shown above may then be the result of problems peculiar to the particular department rather than general shortages. Since there are few or no vacancies in the typist classification, job redesign may be applicable in the sense that some work now the responsibility of stenographers could be alloted to typists, who are in relatively greater supply. Whether clerical work could be so transferred is problematic. Most likely, since duties in this classification are routine, relief from shortages would have to come as the result of better compensation or easing of entrance qualifications.

Table 12

DEPARTMENT OF HEALTH
BUDGETED AND FILLED POSITIONS, FISCAL 1965

Occupational Group or Job Classification	Number of Employees	Budgeted	Vacan-cies
Bacteriology	164	201	37
Chemistry	38	45	7
Public Health Sanitarian	367	722	355
Dental Hygienist	160	183	23
Nutritionists	28	35	7
Public Health Nurse	348	599	251
X-ray Technician	42	45	3
Public Health Assistant	459	543	84
Statistician	31	40	9
TOTAL	1,637	2,413	776

Table 13

DEPARTMENT OF WELFARE
BUDGETED AND FILLED POSITIONS, FISCAL 1965

Occupational Group or Job Classification	Number of Employees	Budgeted	Vacan-cies
Clerical	1,924	2,351	427
Stenographers	691	929	238
Typists	924	1,065	141
Telephone Operators	93	111	18
Attorneys	52	125	73
Senior Accountants	29	39	10
Social Investigators*	4,145	4,435	290
Social Workers	39	60	21
Dental Assistants	47	59	12
TOTAL	7,944	9,174	1,230

*Includes trainees.

94

Table 14

CLERICAL AND STENOGRAPHIC VACANCIES IN
SELECTED CITY DEPARTMENTS, FISCAL 1965

	Number of Vacancies	
Department	Clerical	Stenographic
Hospitals	195	75
Health	16	27
Buildings	46	7
Water Supply	6	3
Parks	16	--
Finance	145	12
Three Library Systems	105	--
TOTAL	529	124

Within the three library systems, New York,
Brooklyn, and Queensborough, the most persistent
shortage is in the various librarian classifications.
The same situation exists nationwide, where it is
estimated that there are currently 5,300 vacancies
in professional librarian positions and that the
shortage may reach 20,000 by 1975.[2] In the City,
there were 73 vacancies during fiscal 1965. Because
the shortage is not particular to the City systems,
this is an area where redesign, if feasible, could
make a significant contribution, whereas other methods such as salary adjustments and recruiting drives
are not likely to be effective in the short run.

In addition to clerical vacancies, the Department of Finance has 65 vacancies in its Accountant
classification of 209 budgeted positions. The Housing and Redevelopment Board has small shortages in
Civil Engineer, Architect, and Planner classifications, although they are large relative to the number
of budgeted positions in those categories. In the
Department of Parks, the largest numbers of vacancies
are among Recreation Leaders, with 75 vacancies of
589 positions; carpenters, 30 vacancies of 77

positions; seasonal parkmen, 50 vacancies of 581 positions; and gardners, 11 vacancies of 175 positions.
The Buildings Department also has shortages in a
number of key positions. As in Housing and Redevelopment, they find it difficult to secure their full
allocation of architects and planners. In addition,
there are shortages of 20 Housing Inspectors and 11
Elevator Inspectors. In the Board of Water Supply,
the major recruiting problem is in the various civil
engineering classifications, where 93 of 365 positions
were vacant during the period surveyed.

MOVEMENT TOWARD JOB REDESIGN

A general shortage of skilled persons is,
naturally, not a problem unique to New York City
government. Unemployment in professional and technical occupations is well below the national average
as is employment in white-collar occupations. Further
employment in professional and technical occupations
is increasing almost twice as fast as is employment
generally. All signs, then, point to continued persistent shortages of skilled employees in the for-
seeable future.

As a result of this pressure on the supply
side, among other things, efforts have been made on
a fairly broad front to apply the concept of job
redesign. The Federal Civil Service Commission, for
example, has established a formal program, Operation
MUST (Maximum Utilization of Skills and Training),
which charges heads of agencies with the responsibility "for making the greatest possible use of job redesign for purposes of economy, improved manpower
utilization, and increased employment opportunities
for the disadvantaged."[3]

Another area where there has been considerable
thought and activity in the application of job redesign and the new careers concept has been in public
assistance and social welfare programs. It is argued by "new careers" proponents that not only are
there social welfare tasks that do not require professional training; in some cases, they can be

performed better by nonprofessionals. This is based
on the notion that middle-class professionals find
it difficult to gain the confidence of lower-class
clients. In addition, it is asserted that indigenous
nonprofessionals have more "know-how" in handling
day-to-day problems with which poor people are con-
fronted, such as budgeting and shopping. As a result,
a number of auxiliary personnel jobs have been proposed, some composed of nonprofessional tasks broken
off from the social worker or social investigator
position and some consisting mainly of tasks not before performed. The various titles are administration aide, research or statistical assistant, welfare
assistant, household helper or home aide, homemaker,
and neighborhood workers. The New York City Department of Welfare has developed a plan to use 4,000
such nonprofessionals over a three-year period, but
the program has been held back because of lack of
funds to finance it.

Similar types of positions have been proposed
for other governmental services. These include--
for schools--family helpers, library aides, school
guides, nursery mothers, school community agents,
talent searchers, and home visitors.[4] In the creation of a teaching ladder, five different functions
have been proposed. The new titles would be teacher
aide, teacher assistant, teacher associate, teacher,
and supervising teacher.[5]

Other services for which new job titles and
descriptions have been proposed include community
mental health programs, research, housing, legal
services, and youth programs.[6]

In the New York City government, relatively
little job redesign has been accomplished. According to the Department of Personnel, it has been considered by a number of agencies; committees were
organized, some studies done, but ultimately formal
programs lapsed. Any changes that have taken place
within departments have been informal; no new titles
have been created, and no entrance qualifications
have been changed.*

----

*As of November, 1966.

One example of an informal restructuring was recently provided by the Police Department when it reassigned 511 policemen from administrative or clerical work to primary police duty. Their replacements included both civilians and police trainees. The latter are between 17 and 21 years of age and receive training in all phases of police work. At age 21, they become eligible for appointment as probationary policemen. Thus, the clerical appointment serves as a first step to ultimate upward movement within the Department's occupational structure. On the other hand, civilians appointed to clerical jobs have no significant promotional opportunities within the Department. It is perhaps for this reason that the Police Commissioner was reported to be making "a special effort to recruit police trainees."[7] In its limited way, the action of the Department represents all of the benefits that can be derived from a "new careers" program. First, it permits more time to be devoted to the duties that can only be performed by the trained policeman. Second, it reduces the cost of providing the clerical services since the trainee's starting pay is $4,000 per year as against $7,032 for patrolmen. Third, career opportunities are opened up for young men who at 17 or 18 years of age might have found it difficult to find career-oriented employment.

JOB REDESIGN FOR NEW YORK CITY

All of these examples--and certainly many others can be provided--point the way to what should be done in every City agency. Although a program similar to that proposed for the Department of Hospitals may be too costly relative to its yield for most departments, at the very minimum, a systematic effort should be made along the lines of the Federal Civil Service program to enlist agency heads, supervisors, and personnel officers in a program to apply job redesign and new career concepts wherever possible. Its general outlines should be formulated by the Department of Personnel, and the Department must adjust its procedures to facilitate the implementation of the program. Resulting changes in job

structure must become formalized into the civil
service structure.

The program should be institutionalized so that
appropriate individuals in each department are charged
with seeing that it is carried out, so that action is
on a continuing basis, and so that the program is coordinated with other training and staffing activities.
There should also be follow-up by agency or Department of Personnel officials, and technical assistance
should be made available in the form of job analysis
techniques, job redesign techniques, information on
available training, and other technical data.   In
this context, the proposed hospital study, if brought
to fruition, should be a rich source of useful material.   The Department of Personnel might also attempt to develop a job redesign indoctrination course
or courses that would be available to all levels of
employees.   The content and time involved would vary
with responsibility for implementation of the program.
For example, middle or lower management might receive
a lengthy detailed course, top management a shorter
one, and workers a fairly simplified one.

Another related problem should be mentioned
here.   The "new careers" idea has as one of its prem-
ises that attention should be paid more to potentialities than past experience or education.   Therefore, one of its by-products would be an easing of
rigid education or experience requirements as well
as a reduction in importance of "certain techniques
such as the ability to fill in questionnaires, to
pass aptitude tests, to use the right words . . .
which may or may not be related to the duties of the
position."[8]

But short of the application of the "new careers" concept, examination of job requirements alone
may pay dividends in easing shortages and providing
job opportunities.   Those found to be unrealistic
should be eased or eliminated.   No attempt has been
made in this study to identify jobs where this is
the case, but it is a reasonable presumption that
they do exist.   The Brookings study, in fact, made
the recommendation that qualification requirements

should be reviewed in order to revise those found to be unrealistic.[9] Recently, <u>The New York Times</u> reported an incident that provided further evidence of inflexible requirements, at least with respect to the department involved. The case involved the dismissal of a young man, provisionally employed as a recreation leader, who had achieved special popularity with the children in a Greenwich Village playground by virtue of his talents as ventriloquist, magician, and puppeteer. His discharge by the Department of Parks was a result of his lacking a college degree, a requirement for permanent employment to the position he had been holding.[10] Although this example may not be representative of all departments, or even of the Department of Parks, entrance requirements should, nevertheless, be scrutinized to identify those that may not be related to the position in question.

It is hazardous to attempt to estimate how many jobs can be created through a systematic program of job redesign; this task necessitates detailed investigation of the occupational structure of each City agency, possibly including job analysis. However, if we can assume that <u>all</u> jobs can be redesigned, then it follows that, under existing budgetary constraints, the number of jobs that could be created would be roughly equal to the existing number of vacancies in professional, technical, and skilled positions. We have no exact count of these, but, on the basis of 3,000 professional and technical vacancies in the departments of Hospitals and Health and significant numbers in the departments of Finance, Parks, Buildings, Water Supply, Housing and Redevelopment, Highways, and Public Works, 10,000 career positions seems a reasonable estimate. And if additional financing were available, certainly 25,000 jobs, on the evidence of the Greenleigh study, could be created in a relatively short period of time.[11]

Some further word about financing is in order here. It seems clear that a considerable number of jobs can be created for the poor through job redesign within the structure of existing budgets. In addition, a number of new positions will result from

increased expenditures financed by expanding tax
revenues and expected increases in state and Federal
aid. On the other hand, if we expect to be able to
create a much larger number of career opportunities
in the City government in order to radically improve
the quality and quantity of services and to be able
to provide employment to anyone who cannot find a
job elsewhere, massive increases in Federal financing
must be forthcoming. The Scheuer-Nelson Amendment
is, of course, a start in this direction, but it needs
to be expanded many, many times before it can enable
local governments and nonprofit institutions to act
as "employers of last resort" as suggested by the
President's Commission of Technology and the American Economy.[12] An example of the kinds of sums that
would be involved was given by Frank Riessman. He
estimates that it would cost about $5 billion per
year, including training, to finance 1 million nonprofessional jobs.[13] The Scheuer-Nelson program
provided only $33 million in its initial year.

It should be clearly understood that these
Federally financed jobs are in fact jobs, not dis-
guised doles. The list of unmet urban needs is
great; there is hardly a service that is not defi-
cient, whether pollution control, police protection,
hospitals, health clinics, schools, or parks. Not
only will new jobs help in the improvement of these
services, they will help in the full development of
human resources both economically and culturally.
The benefits of social and economic integration of
disadvantaged groups long outside of the mainstream
of society are immeasurable. Certainly the human
cost of unemployment and isolation must, by present-
day standards, be judged to be greater than any economic inefficiency connected with subsidized employment. And certainly in a society that has not served
the moral connection between work and the right to
income, job creation must be considered superior to
a guaranteed income and most certainly to existing
welfare programs as a means of easing and ultimately
eliminating poverty.

Redesigning jobs on a systematic and large-
scale basis will be a complicated and at times

frustrating task, as will be the application of the
"new careers" concept to the resulting occupational
structure. But the rewards in expanding public employment and career opportunity can be great. Enough
work has been done in this area to enable the merit
of the scheme to be recognized; it now remains for
the New York City government to give it what can be
its largest and most significant opportunity.

NOTES

1. David T. Stanley, et al., Professional
Personnel for the City of New York (Washington,
D.C.: The Brookings Institution, 1963), pp. 28-29.

2. The New York Times, May 30, 1967.

3. Civil Service Bulletin, No. 300-11, December 23, 1966.

4. Arthur Pearl and Frank Riessman, New Careers
for the Poor (New York: Free Press, 1965), pp. 48-49.

5. Ibid., p. 57.

6. Ibid., Ch. 5 and 6, and Appendix.

7. The New York Times, April 2, 1967.

8. Oscar Ornati, Poverty Amid Affluence (New
York: Twentieth Century Fund, 1966), p. 85.

9. Stanley, op. cit., p. 223.

10. The New York Times, October 2, 1966.

11. Greenleigh Associates, Inc., "Potential
for a Federally-Financed Community Employment Program for the Unemployed Poor in New York City," New
York, November, 1966. This survey covered 27 municipal and state agencies and 36 voluntary, nonprofit
agencies in New York City. These agencies estimated
that over 35,000 nonprofessional jobs could be created

under a Federally-financed community employment program. City agencies accounted for almost 25,000 of
these, with almost 2,000 of the City jobs provided
by the Department of Hospitals. The accuracy of
this survey is limited by the fact that not all agencies were covered or able to supply estimates and
that the jobs, for the most part, were expansions of
job categories that already existed in the agencies.
On the other hand, the estimates go beyond unfilled
vacancies in that they include jobs that would "contribute to improving or extending the Agencies'
services."

        12. Technology and the American Economy,
Report of the National Commission on Technology,
Automation and Economic Progress (Washington, D.C.:
U.S. Government Printing Office, 1966), p. 37.

        13. "The New Careers Concept," American Child,
Vol. 49, No. 1 (Winter, 1967), p. 32.

APPENDIX

APPENDIX

Veteran's Administration Nursing Activity Classification Code

0. Waiting Time:

    0.1 Waiting during Ministration of Direct Nursing Care.
    0.2 Waiting for Report, or during Indirect Nursing Care.
    0.3 Waiting for Reasons of Security.
    0.4 Waiting for Professional Personnel or Professional Services.
    0.5 Waiting for Hospital Technical Personnel, Supplies or Services.
    0.6 Waiting for Institutional Personnel, Supplies or Services.
    0.7 Waiting for Personnel Services, Supplies or Personnel.
    0.8
    0.9 Waiting for Reasons other than the above.

1. Direct Nursing Care--Activities directly with an individual patient, patient and family, or group of patients.

    1.1 Ministering to Physical Needs and Mental Hygiene.
    1.2 Ministering to Psychosocial Needs and Mental Hygiene.
    1.3 Observing Signs, Symptoms, Reactions.
    1.4 Administering or Assisting with Administration of Tests, Medicines, Treatments.
    1.5 Teaching Patient and/or Family.
    1.6 Supervising Patient Practice in Prescribed Activities.
    1.7 Planning with Patient and/or Family.

1.8   Patient Transport Service.
1.9   Other, or Nonrecurring Activities with
      Patient.

2.   Indirect Nursing Care: Activities <u>done away</u>
     from patients, but part of preparation, plan-
     ning, completing their total nursing care.

2.1   Providing for Physical Care and Personal
      Hygiene.
2.2   Providing for Emotional Care and Mental
      Hygiene.
2.3   Communicating Patient's Condition and/or
      Nursing Care Between or Among Nursing
      Personnel in the Unit.
2.4   Providing for Administration of Tests,
      Treatments or Medicines.
2.5   Providing for Patient Teaching.
2.6   Supervising Nursing Care.
2.7
2.8
2.9   Other, or Nonrecurring Activities for the
      Patient.

3.   Security for All: Activities for safety and
     protection of all persons and property; check-
     ing, inspecting, counting, safeguarding,
     locking.

3.1   Protecting Patient.
3.2   Protecting Patient's Property.
3.3
3.4   Medical-Legal Activities.
3.5   Safety Teaching.
3.6   Safety Supervision.
3.7   Administration and Planning for Safety
      and Protection.
3.8   Escorting for Protection.
3.9   Other Security Activities.

4.   Coordinating Professional Services: Activities
     in operating the Nursing Service; in implement-
     ing the nursing part of the total therapeutic
     regimen for patients or coordinating it with
     professional services.

4.1 Nursing Service (within nursing).
4.2 Diet Therapy (but not Food Service,
     see 6.2).
4.3 Physical Medicine and Rehabilitation.
4.4 Medical Services.
4.5 Social Work Service.
4.6 Chaplain Service.
4.7 Administration and Planning Interdepart-
     mental Operations.
4.8 Dental Service.
4.9 Operating Room Services.

5. Coordinating Hospital Technical Services:
    Activities in coordinating and/or obtaining
    hospital technical services and supplies for
    patients.

    5.1 Laboratory Service Including Blood Bank.
    5.2 Volunteer Services.
    5.3 X-ray Service Including Radiation Therapy.
    5.4 Pharmaceutical Service.
    5.5 Sterilizing Service (but not Supply
         Service, see 6.9).
    5.6 Barber Service.
    5.7 Administration and Planning Interdepart-
         mental Operations.
    5.8 Transport and Escort Service (but not
         Patient Transport Service, see 1.8, or
         Personnel Travel, see 7.8).
    5.9 Registrar Service.

6. Coordinating Institutional Services: Activities
    in coordinating and/or obtaining institutional
    services and supplies for all persons.

    6.1 Housekeeping Service.
    6.2 Food Service (but not Diet Therapy, see
         4.2).
    6.3 Clerical Service.
    6.4 Fiscal Service.
    6.5 Laundry Service.
    6.6
    6.7 Administration and Planning Interdepart-
         mental Operations.
    6.8 Engineering Service.

6.9 Supply Service (but not Sterilizing
     Service, see 5.5).

7.   Personnel Services: Activities in providing
     services to nursing personnel--individuals
     or groups.

7.1 Personnel Services.
7.2 Timekeeping and Payment.
7.3 Employment Activities.
7.4 Personnel Health Services.
7.5 Inservice Training of Nursing Assistants
     and/or Practical Nurses.
7.6 Staff Education of Professional Nurses.
7.7 Administration and Planning for Personnel
     Services.
7.8 Personnel Travel (but not Patient Trans-
     port Service, see 1.8).
7.9 Activities in Providing Nonrecurring
     Services.

Source: Veteran's Administration, Program Guide:
For Studying the Utilization of Nursing
Service Personnel in Veterans Administration
Hospitals, G-7, M-2, Part V, Department of
Medicine and Surgery (Washington, D.C.:
March 30, 1961), Ch. 2, pp. 12-14.

BIBLIOGRAPHY

BIBLIOGRAPHY

Atkeson, Paula, "Alternative Career Opportunities for the Neighborhood Worker," Social Work, Vol. 12, No. 4 (October, 1967).

Blum, Arthur, "Differential Use of Manpower in Public Welfare," Social Work, Vol. 11, No. 1 (January, 1966).

Education for the Allied Health Professions and Services. (Public Health Service, U.S. Department of Health, Education, and Welfare.) Washington, D.C.: U.S. Government Printing Office, 1967.

Employment Service Review, November, 1966. Entire edition on "Health Manpower."

Fine, Sidney A., "A Re-examination of Transferability of Skills," Monthly Labor Review, August, 1957.

Fry, Hilary, in collaboration with William P. Shepard and Ray H. Elling. Education and Manpower for Community Health. Pittsburgh, Pa.: University of Pittsburgh Press, 1967.

Hellman, Louis M., and O'Brien, Francis B., "Nurse Midwifery--An Experiment in Maternity Care," Obstetrics and Gynecology, Vol. 24, No. 3 (September, 1964).

Job Redesign for Older Workers: Ten Case Studies. U.S. Department of Labor, Office of Manpower Policy, Evaluation and Research and Bureau of Labor Statistics, Bulletin No. 1523.

Levinson, Perry, and Schiller, Jeffry, "Role
     Analysis of the Indigenous Non-Professional,"
     Social Work, Vol. 11, No. 3 (July, 1966).

Mirengoff, William, "Health Manpower--An Emerging
     Challenge," Employment Service Review,
     November, 1966.

National Commission on Community Health Services.
     Health is a Community Affair. Cambridge, Mass.:
     Harvard University Press, 1966.

New Careers Newsletter. New York: New Careers De-
     velopment Center, New York University.

"The New Non-Professional," American Child, Vol. 49,
     No. 1 (Winter, 1967). Articles by Frank
     Riessman, Edith F. Lynton, Sherman Barr, and
     Mark Battle. Forum with Mitchell Ginsberg,
     Brendan Sexton, Frank Riessman, Eli E. Cohen,
     and Seymour Lesh.

Pearl, Arthur, and Riessman, Frank, New Careers for
     the Poor. New York: Free Press, 1965.

Prager, Robert, and Specht, Harry, "Establishing New
     Careers Programs: Organizational Barriers and
     Strategies," Social Work, Vol. 13, No. 4
     (October, 1968).

Richan, W. C., "A Theoretical Scheme for Determining
     Roles of Professional and Non-Professional
     Personnel," Social Work, Vol. 6 (October, 1961).

Riessman, Frank, "The Coming Revolution in Social
     Service," Trans-Action, November-December, 1964.

Riessman, Frank, and Popper, Hermine L., Up From
     Poverty. New York: Harper and Row, 1968.

Rothberg, Herman J., "Job Redesign for Older Workers:
     Case Studies," Monthly Labor Review, January,
     1967.

Stanley, David T., et al., Professional Personnel
     for the City of New York. Washington, D.C.:
     The Brookings Institution, 1963.

Sturm, Herman M., "Technological Developments and
     Their Effects Upon Health Manpower," Monthly
     Labor Review, January, 1967.

Summary of Proceedings: Workshop on Non-Professional
     Careers for Disadvantaged Youth. New York:
     Center for the Study of Unemployed Youth,
     Graduate School of Social Work, New York Uni-
     versity, 1966.

Technicians for the Health Field: A Community
     College Health Careers Study Program. New
     York: University of the State of New York,
     State Education Department, 1966.

Thompson, Jane K., and Riley, Donald P., "Use of
     Professionals in Public Welfare: A Dilemma
     and a Proposal," Social Work, Vol. 11, No. 1
     (January, 1966).

Training the Auxiliary Health Worker: An Analysis
     of Functions, Training Content, Training Costs
     and Facilities. (Public Health Service, U.S.
     Department of Health, Education, and Welfare.)
     Washington, D.C.: U.S. Government Printing
     Office, 1968.

Weed, Verne, and Denham, William H., "Toward More
     Effective Use of the Non-Professional Worker:
     A Recent Experiment," Social Work, Vol. 6,
     No. 4, pp. 29-36.

ABOUT THE AUTHOR

Mark A. Haskell, Associate Professor of Public Finance at New York University Graduate School of Public Administration, is a specialist both in labor economics and in public finance and administration. His articles have appeared in the <u>National Tax Journal</u> and other publications, and he has acted as an arbiter in labor disputes. In addition, he has recently participated in tax studies for the cities of New York and San Francisco and for the state of Hawaii.

Professor Haskell was formerly on the staffs of Rutgers University and Queens College and held a Fulbright scholarship in Australia. He studied at Cornell and Rutgers universities and was granted his Ph.D. by the latter institution.